The Spoken Word

FORTRESS RESOURCES FOR PREACHING

Daniel Patte, *Preaching Paul*
Robert G. Hughes, *A Trumpet in Darkness*
Bernard Brandon Scott, *The Word of God in Words*
John Blackwell, *The Passion as Story*
Donald Macleod, *The Problem of Preaching*
John Mason Stapleton, *Preaching in Demonstration
of the Spirit and Power*
David G. Buttrick, *Preaching Jesus Christ*
Richard L. Thulin, *The "I" of the Sermon*

The Spoken Word

SHELDON A. TOSTENGARD

FORTRESS PRESS   MINNEAPOLIS

Library of Congress Cataloging-in-Publication Data

Tostengard, Sheldon A.
    The spoken word.

    (Fortress resources for preaching)
    Bibliography: p.
    1. Languages—Religious aspects—Christianity.
2. Preaching. I. Title. II. Series.
    BR115.L25T67 1989   251   88–45229
    ISBN 0–8006–1149–7

3450I88   Printed in the United States of America   1–1149

For Dorothy
whose persistent
lack of interest in theology has
refreshed our marriage

Contents

Preface   9

1. The Church and the Problem of Language   13

2. Words and the Word in Our Culture   26

3. The Resources   47
   Part 1. Theological: Luther and the Word
   Part 2. Biblical: Words and the Word in the Bible
   Part 3. Interpretive: Language and Interpretation

4. The Word in the Church's Life   82
   Part 1. The Problem of Language and Christian Worship
   Part 2. Words, the Word, and Preaching

Conclusion   105

Notes   107

Preface

Preaching is a sacred calling and the preparation and delivery of sermons is, on the one hand, beyond instruction, a matter of prayer and the work of the Holy Spirit. On the other hand, preaching is a very human work, a craft that demands our utmost discipline and creativity. One Sunday after another marches up to the preacher in what seems an endless, relentless procession, and people really do come to hear, eager for some word of truth, of hope, of freedom. Little wonder that most preachers long for encouragement and advice about their sermons.

God provides the only sure and certain encouragement for preaching. God has called us to preach and we do well to remember that calling and to draw strength from it. We are also sometimes allowed to overhear the gospel that we are preaching, and our own faith is thereby strengthened. Even the encouragement of completing a creative task can be understood as a gift of God, although seasoned preachers learn to be wary of that Sunday afternoon feeling of satisfaction, knowing that feelings can lie to us. God lifts us up in our preaching—sometimes even by our own sermons—and the best testimony to God's protection of the preacher is the simple fact that pastors continue to prepare sermons faithfully and to tell the story of Jesus clearly and eloquently throughout our land.

This book seeks to provide another form of encouragement for preaching, one from the more wordly perspectives of theology and a particular understanding of language. If the great impediment to our preaching is our own unbelief, a lesser but gnawing dilemma grows out of the sense that our human words, primarily in oral form, are the tools of our trade. We are people who speak in a world where language is much depreciated, especially in its oral form. We are people who speak in a world which believes deep in the marrow of its cognitive bones that talk is cheap; not that talk might be cheap, or hurtful, or damaging, but that talk is, in its being, plain cheap. All around us are slick professionals possessed of the facile tools of their trades—machines, clever advertisements, the oak- and velvet-bound tradition of the law—while we have only our simple words. It's discouraging! One of my colleagues, with wry and self-effacing humor, claims that as ballplayers insure their arms and dancers insure their legs, we should insure our mouths. Preachers cannot help but wonder if Christ has chosen to come to us as the Word in our words simply to show that God can do anything.

We shall attempt to show, however, that it makes sense that Christ comes to us in that most characteristic, direct and yet hidden, intimate form of communion that we possess, our human words to each other. God cannot be seen, not even by the cosmonauts speeding through the heavenly vaults, but God can be heard, heard in our mortal words. Resources in our theological tradition contend that it is so, as do resources in the Bible and in certain cultural studies of language: the same primeval voice of God that gave shape to boulders and wings to gulls, that word that has come to us in these latter days as Jesus, now waits to take form in our own mouths. What better way for our Lord to draw near us and change us. The scandal of our preaching is not that Jesus comes in our weakness, for he is the carpenter's son, but that it is the saving Christ who comes to us. In the face of all sorts of more fundamental discouragements, it is encouraging for the preacher to know that his or her own words are just the right tools for the gospel.

The advice which we propose for the practical tasks of preaching grows out of this encouragement. Learning to treasure the spoken word again because of our faith in a speaking God teaches us some things about how language is to be used in worship and, more particularly, in sermons. From the very beginning of the weekly homiletical task, when the pastor first reads the text, to the end, when the sermon is delivered, we are instructed as well as encouraged by our understanding of the nature and power of language. For instance, a sense for the living character of language may make interpretation more of a productive and lively adventure or a sense for forms of discourse most closely connected to orality may help us to compose our sermons with material best suited to the intimate, compelling, demanding, surprising, saving news of the gospel.

I wish to thank the Aid Association for Lutherans, Lutheran Brotherhood, and the president and board of Luther Northwestern Seminary for helping to provide the occasion for researching, planning, and writing this book.

SHELDON A. TOSTENGARD
Luther Northwestern Seminary

1
The Church and the Problem of Language

'My nerves are bad tonight. Yes, bad. Stay with me.
'Speak to me. Why do you never speak. Speak.
'What are you thinking of? What thinking? What?
'I never know what you are thinking. Think.'
                          T. S. Eliot, *The Wasteland*, pt. II

Not long ago I visited a huge and historic cathedral church. It is a beautiful building, especially the windows. As I walked quietly about the great vault, those windows filled my path with dappled splendor. Above all, it was utterly quiet. Just once, off in an unseen corner, I heard a woman's heels clicking on the stone. Then she was gone and the quiet returned. That church is mostly a mausoleum now, the abode of many dead and the last resting place of forgotten hymns. If you were to linger in the silence long enough, it might be that a great loneliness would come over you—not a sense of being alone with God, but just a sad sense of being utterly, completely alone. It's the silence that does it—that eerie, dead silence.

THE CHURCH AS AN ORAL COMMUNITY

Martin Luther, for instance, wouldn't have liked a silent church. He couldn't imagine a church without sound—in particular, the sound of the gospel being proclaimed and believers responding with prayer and praise. Christians believe and confess that the church is called forth and sustained by the Word of God.

Luther himself had a simple, yet profound idea about the Word of God. *Word*, for him, was preeminently the spoken word of the gospel

13

of Jesus, a word spoken with the mouth and heard with the ear. The gospel is the good news of Jesus' saving work for us, and there just isn't any better way to deliver good news than with an announcement, face to face. Luther also considered the sacraments, which are means of grace and constitutive of the church, to be communication events. They are words of the gospel in, with, and under the elements of water, bread, and wine.

The spoken word is appropriate for the gospel because the gospel is immediate, arresting, and something that we cannot control. The spoken word is also appropriate to the believing hearer, for the message of the gospel must finally be "written" on the heart. Writing on the heart is usually done by language. There is freedom for grace in the spoken word too, for who knows just how a word will be heard or responded to. Jesus is hidden within the freedom and ordinariness of language, hidden there until the Spirit makes him known. To be sure, the written word can also become the living word of faith for a believer. But it is preeminently the spoken word, spoken in the name of Jesus, that calls forth and sustains the church.

Luther would not have liked that silent church which housed so many dead people. He would have wanted some sound in there, the sound of the speaking of the gospel and of a response of prayer and praise. The gospel is the news of the saving work of our risen and present Lord Jesus. It is news of and from a person, news which is most appropriately conveyed in the living voice of speech.

For Luther, the church is an oral community, a group of people gathered to hear the gospel and speak it to the world. The church is not the repository of information about God, but a community which experiences the present Christ in word and sacrament, and shares Christ with the world.

Talk of hearing and speaking may suggest an absence of genuine work, as though the gospel is not really done among us and as though Christians don't really enact the gospel in the world. The modern dichotomy between speaking and acting is a false one. Speaking, of course, is our most typical action, and one cannot imagine nonverbal actions apart from the context of language. For example, does the beloved to whom a word of love has been spoken usually suspect that word of being something other than the action of love? And is it possible that the acts of charity in behalf of the beloved can exist without any word?

Luther called the church a "mouth-house" rather than a "pen-house." He taught the Scriptures and had the deepest reverence for them. Nevertheless, his sense for the church as an oral community was so strong that he regretted that the gospels ever had to be written down. Of course, he knew very well that it was a blessing that they had been written down so that they could not be lost or badly altered. But Luther longed for the spoken, living word. Gerhard Ebeling writes of Luther:

> This concentration on the true substance of the gospel is directly related to a concentration upon oral preaching. For "the gospel ought not really to be written, but should be a spoken word. . . . That is why Christ himself wrote nothing, but only spoke, and why his teaching is not called scripture, but the gospel, that is, the good news or preaching, which ought not to be proclaimed with the pen, but with the spoken word." That the gospel should be given a fixed written form is basically inappropriate, and is at best the result of necessity. "That it was necessary to write books is in itself a great breach and decline from the spirit: it was caused by necessity and is not the proper nature of the New Testament." Thus when Luther speaks of the gospel, he is referring strictly and exclusively to the Christian proclamation, which, although it depends upon the biblical text for the testimony which provides its norm, is enabled to testify on this basis at the present day; and without this the gospel would not be put into effect as such.[1]

The key to understanding the church as an oral community is to understand the nature of the gospel as an event. Luther certainly understood it to be so. The gospel is an aggressive word, a word that invades our privacy and calls our life into question. The gospel is an urgent word in announcing that the time is at hand, that this very day is the day for repentance. The gospel is an unqualified word, the announcement that there is nothing that can shake us from the hand of God's love. The word of the gospel is an event—an encounter which is always complete, once and for all, but which is also daily and ever new. With the gospel word there is no time for meditation, for putting our thoughts in order. With that word there is no engraved invitation that can be considered or even stored away. With that word there is no private vision of angels and archangels and all the company of heaven. The Word of God is the complete, the stark, the arresting, the blessed but simple: "Come unto me all ye that labor, and I will give you rest." The gospel is an event, an occurrence on which the church is built and our own faith depends. The gospel is not about Jesus; it is Jesus. The gospel is not about love; it is love. The gospel is not about freedom, for with the very word of Jesus the believing hearer is set free. The immediacy of the gospel event is best conveyed by the immediacy of speech.

To emphasize speaking and hearing in the community of the church is by no means to deemphasize other human senses. The church is the living body of Christ and comes into full and complete human contact with the world. Sight is important to our worship. To see the empty cross, beautiful windows telling Bible stories, or friends in the congregation contributes to the life of worship. To touch and taste the bread and the wine—those elements of the earth which now, under the promise of Christ, have become the very means of grace—is central to Christian living. Even smell is important—the smell of candles burning, or of food being cooked in the basement of a country church, or of the lilies on Easter morning. Even some Protestants confess to having been intrigued by the sweet smell of churchly incense now and then.

The sacraments are clear evidence that it is our Lord's intention that all our senses be awakened in worship. Nevertheless, the church is preeminently an oral community. The spoken word of the gospel is the life's breath of that body. It is very much like a family gathering for a festive meal. The house is decorated with lovely, appropriate colors, and the table is beautifully set, a sign of what is to come. Familiar, precious faces gather around, and familiar, delightful smells drift in from the kitchen. Can you imagine such a meal if speech were prohibited? There is plenty of talk, you can be sure of that. One person can hardly wait to visit with another. One or two may be uneasy at the prospect of a visit with a certain other. Talk is the key to the gathering; and if, for a moment, there should be silence, it could only be out of respect for someone who has died or in prayer for some greater word from beyond.

LANGUAGE AS THE
CRISIS OF THE CHURCH

There is a crisis in and for the church these days, a crisis deeper and larger than any temporary antidote which a conservative climate of opinion might offer. It is a crisis which is palpable and obvious in Europe and America. Ernst Käsemann writes:

> For something is happening now which in my judgment has never happened before. When we speak in our day of ecumenism and mission, we have always in front of our eyes the picture of a church extending throughout the world which is going on growing even in spite of bad setbacks. This picture, at least taken in isolation, is false or even merely the deceptive superficial appearance of a highly alarming reality. It seems to me that we ought rather to be seeing Christendom under the sign of a worldwide dying and of closing doors. [2]

Although Christians can rejoice over the vitality of the church in parts of Africa, Asia, and South America, there can be little doubt that in the West, for the first time, the church is swimming against the stream. One cannot help but wonder if the church is not moving, however gradually, in the direction of that great mausoleum of the dead which is a magnificent relic of a former age but is now bereft of life and totally silent.

Christians sense the crisis of the church in their bones. Church leaders see it, pastors feel it, lay folks know it is so. With characteristic American vigor, and without trying very hard to determine from a theological perspective just what the nature of the crisis is, we set out to do something about it. Thoughtless, headlong action just makes everything worse. Bureaucratic efficiency, pastoral therapy or managerial skill, and congregational aggressiveness have just compounded the dilemma.

Careful thought and prayer are needed along two lines. On the one hand, as Käsemann rightly observes, Christians need to quit trying to save the church. The preservation of the church is God's business, and God will be sure to carry it out. To try to save the church is to forget that the church is Christ's body in our world, a body that we have not established and one which we shall not be able to destroy. The church will be preserved, make no mistake about that, but we pray that it might also be preserved unto us. As Käsemann suggests, the question for the Christian in the face of the dwindling of the church is never, "How can I save the church?" but rather, "What does it mean for the church, and for me, to be a disciple of Jesus just now?"

On the other hand, Christians need to consider what might be at the heart of the crisis of the churches. Certainly there are many contributing factors: the unfortunate linkage of church and state which began with the emperor Constantine (A.D. 313) and has taken various forms; the identification between the church and certain utopian dreams which have proven to be false; the business success of Christians and the church, which has tended to make many denominations hopelessly middle class and far from the needs and virtues of the poor. The list could go on and on, as various as the manifestations of sin. But the crisis of the church is, above all, a crisis of the word, a crisis of language.

A crisis of the church is always rooted in some form of unbelief. The crisis of language is no exception. It is a failure to believe that God will come to us as promised, a failure to believe that there will be any saving word from beyond, a failure to believe that the distant God can draw near to us, as near as our hearing. It is a failure to believe in a present God, a God who is at hand. The language crisis is rooted in a failure to believe in Jesus, the One who still wishes to speak a word of love and mercy to us. Belief in a God who is an abstract principle, often the last mental resort of those who have become disenchanted with the church, is sadly amusing. What is such a God like? How will such a God become known to us? What difference will such a God make when the earth is shaking beneath our very feet? Unbelief in God must always be at the point of revelation, at the point where God becomes a part of our world.

From the Christian perspective, unbelief is always unbelief in Jesus Christ, in his presence among us. Jesus is the Word of God. The crisis of the church is the suspicion that there cannot be any word from beyond, any word of Jesus to set us into action with hope, any word from beyond to set us free. If some word of hope and freedom does come, it is assumed that it will only be the word of a dreaming church, not the voice of a holy God. The question of our time is not whether Jesus *will* speak; that is already a form of faith. The question is whether Jesus *can* speak or is utterly, magnificently silent.

The church has always lived on the edge of a language crisis; but in our time there is a particular situation in the world, a particular characteristic of culture which makes the normal problem of faith and language much worse. It is the general disparagement of language, particularly in its spoken form, which exists throughout society. Speech is simply not thought to be a high form of communication, and the spoken word is not held to be a lively bearer of the truth. A combination of numbers, or even the printed word, may very well hold the truth; but speech is thought to be too ordinary, too ephemeral to be relied upon. It's not that we have quit using speech in our daily lives; we do that as much or more than ever before. But we don't associate speech with the objective truths which are "out there," except as a necessary vehicle to convey information about them. Speech is thought to convey facts, sentiments, and ideas in the same way that an empty box conveys an article placed in it.

THE DEATH OF LANGUAGE

So widespread is our devaluation of language, particularly in its spoken form, that the death of language has become accepted. Nearly all of us would agree that "actions speak louder than words." That, we would say, is self-evident. Consider what is being said here. Words, for one thing, are not considered to be actions. Actions are thought to be objective, visible, real, capable of changing the course of life. Words are of a second and lesser class: invisible, fleeting, and often subject to various interpretations. Yet, as though some primal knowledge of the power of speech is lurking within, actions are given the qualities which speech normally has; they "speak loudly," more loudly than words.

"Talk is cheap" is another axiom most of us would subscribe to. Consider again what the meaning is for language. Clearly it is the spoken word that is the enemy here. "Talk" does not refer to the printed word but most certainly to that communion which is achieved through human speaking and hearing. The word "is" looms as all inclusive. No allowance is made for the different effect a spoken word might have. For example, this axiom does not carry the obvious meaning that the spoken word is sometimes harmful and damaging. No, speech is given a neutral category, the necessary container which is just "cheap." After all, "Sticks and stones can break my bones, but words will never hurt me."

To say that we are living in the time of the death of language is to make a massive claim, particularly when language in its written form is being stored up as never before. Books abound, and no sooner does one become popular among readers than it is replaced by another. Computers are the supreme repositories of print, and word processors manage our words with a speed and accuracy that no human could manage. There are also greater opportunities for oral exchange than ever before. People can speak on the telephone, and the speed and ease of modern travel makes face-to-face communication increasingly common. Yet, in spite of all the language around us, our society does believe that "talk is cheap" and that "actions speak louder than words."

Society willingly, eagerly embraces and contributes to the death of language without stopping to think of what the consequences might be. Language does not live and thrive simply because there is a lot of talk and a lot of print. Language dies when we don't cherish the spoken word and split it away from the written, visible word. Orality is prior to and more important than the printed word. The word in the world of sound, both historically and in our everyday lives, comes before the printed word. Now, however, the visible word, fixed in space, giving the illusion of being the objective truth "out there," has completely won the day. Once it stands written it seems to us to be true. The ephemeral, mysterious spoken word, which is already gone as soon as it is spoken, is of a secondary and lesser class.

The modern scientific era is the age of sight, not of sound. "Seeing is believing." It is that sight-sound split which is at the heart of the death of language. The visible, printed word is split away, in our thinking, from the spoken word, and printed words are given greater truth-bearing value than speech. Both the printed and the spoken word suffer—the spoken word by simply being devalued, and the printed word by being robbed of oral liveliness and urgency. The church, which has as its business to wait upon and speak the word of Jesus, suffers too.

Language is that which most properly separates people from the beasts. It is so intimately and personally related to our being that what we expect of language is what we get. If we expect that the oral word will be a vessel for truth but not truth itself, or a container for an attitude rather than its enactment, speech will become boring, second class, and flat. The freedom, beauty, and communal nature of oral discourse will, to some extent, be lost. The death of language, particularly in the form of the death of oral discourse, is more than a misplaced private option; it is a tragedy of our life together, a terrible rent in the fabric of community.

Seeing is something that a person does alone. The printed word is available to our solitary vision, whereas speaking and hearing is a communal affair. We are not meant to be alone, and our capacity to speak to and listen for one another is constitutive of the family of humankind. The oral word is not a characteristic of family life; it creates and sustains family life.

Speech gains its currency from the everyday, down-to-earth experiences of life. Language can become sophisticated, but if it is to have meaning, then it has to be rooted in experience. Consider three lines from one of Gerard Manley Hopkins's beautiful poems:

Glory to God for dappled things
For skies of couple-colour as a brindled cow:
For rose-moles all in stipple upon trout that swim:[3]

Although these lines are primarily visual in orientation, the concrete character of language is readily apparent. Hopkins had looked long at a dappled sky and had seen more than one tawny, mottled cow. He had seen roses and imagined them scattered, glistening and tremulous, upon the swimming trout. To those who read with sensitivity and have had somewhat similar experiences, these words can re-create the past and set the spirit soaring. The words create a new event, better than the former vision, for the former vision has been given a name, a name which has about it the ring of truth. It is strange how language can surpass the visual event when words and experience are well knit together. Of course, these are printed lines, but poets still like to speak their words.

When language is cut loose from experience, however, it loses specificity and begins to die. Because words are the heartbeat of our life together, community begins to suffer as well. When the oral word is conceived of as a container without its own content, it is bound to be divorced from the vivid, urgent experience that composes our existence. Words, although they can only exist as generalities, become utterly general, with vague attachments to broad and typical aspects of life. Gerhard Ebeling has written that the language crisis "lies in the fact that the coherent structure of understanding has broken down, because language has taken on an existence of its own and has become isolated from its basis in experience. Consequently the words are uttered into a void, their universality becomes universality and nothing more. They are no longer in touch with the concrete and treat it as hostile."[4] Words, in order to communicate, must be general enough to include a class of instances but specific enough to be rooted in concrete life. The lack of capacity for concretization is typical, in our time, of words that are dying.

A good example of the death of the oral word, and one filled with particular irony, revolves around the word *wellness*. It is a word often used these days by people who are rightly concerned with the health of the total person. For too long we have been preoccupied with the empirical, visible aspects of life at the expense of the emotional and spiritual. (Even to speak those words suggests a separation which is very difficult to discern.) Nevertheless, however well intentioned, people interested in the health of the total organism are cheated by a dying language. *Wellness* will just not do, and it will not do because it is utterly general, completely airborne. *Wellness*, as a word, has to come down somewhere in experience; it has to have some location. A well person has to get rid of a skin rash, or a persistent depression, or a pathological fear of even moderately small places. To suggest to a purveyor of "wellness" that the process begin with the removal of some warts would not only show the language to be general but arrogant in the extreme.

Our language is full of soaring, vacuous generalities—words that don't touch down anywhere. They are the antiphon of a fellowship that is slipping away. Who would deny that ours is a world filled with sound and chatter but a world which also tends toward boredom and loneliness? Eliot's lines makes a suitable epitaph for our time:

'My nerves are bad tonight. Yes, bad. Stay with me.
'Speak to me. Why do you never speak. Speak.'

Please be clear that the decay of the oral word does not merely diminish our capacity to describe experience but actually robs us of life together. Language is not only the symptom of community, it is also its bearer. When the spoken word becomes divorced from life, it contributes to a vicious circle whereby both language and life are impoverished. So, when our words do not have meaning, our life does not have meaning. "I am thinking of a fact, all too familiar, that a great expenditure of words can often result in little or nothing being said. Discourse turns into chatter. Language becomes mere form without content. When language is drained of meaning in this way, it is probably a sign that the speaker himself is as it were drained of meaning."[5]

Society, of course, always manages to find one way or another to be ill. One or more aspects of our culture always need healing. But the sickness of language is not one social disease among others. Rather, it is a sickness of the heart, a sickness unto death.

THE PROBLEM OF LANGUAGE
AS A RELIGIOUS PROBLEM

The problem of language is a religious problem, a manifestation of sin. Its roots are in our age-old preoccupation with ourselves—our desire to stand alone, to be autonomous, to be like God. In modern times, the human drive toward autonomy has taken two forms which are particularly related to the problem of language: the desire to see causality (the reason why things happen), and the search for individual freedom (the desire to be in control).

Vision perceives events as happening in sequence. Events, with the exception of occasional mutations, are the predictable result of their antecedent causes. The occasions of life appear to be like a row of dominoes, each one standing on its own but each determined by the action of its cause. Vision allows us to see what we want to believe— that life is not only predictable but controllable as well.

The oral-aural word does not readily give the impression of sequentiality but of a contemporary, complete event. Hearing apprehends occasions as novel and surprising. Babies are filled with wonder at the sounds around them: the squeak of a rocking chair, the sharp report of a fallen object, the soft sound of a parental voice. Our devotion to causality has provided us with many blessings, but it has robbed us of wonder. God is still the creator. Vision shows us that God creates life after its own kind, but it is hearing that apprehends the creation as truly new.

Vision is a solitary matter, something that one does alone. Certainly a primary characteristic of sin in our time is a wanton privatization of needs, rights, and responsibilities. We want to "do our own thing," "get in touch with our feelings," and "take control of our own destiny." Our pathological preoccupation with individuality is sponsored by our fascination with the visual. God has made each person wonderfully unique. Can there be any parents who haven't wondered at the strange mystery of individuality which unfolds in the life of one who is also bone of their bone and flesh of their flesh? Nevertheless, privatization of needs, rights, and responsibilities leads to a delusion which runs contrary to the nature of God's intention for us. It is sin. God is love and intends that we love our neighbor, a calling which is communal rather than private. Speaking and hearing is something that we do together. The oral-aural world does not give an austere, isolated freedom, but is congenial with a true freedom within the dependence and belonging of community. Seeing something truly beautiful is a great blessing, but any child knows that those moments are best when shared with another through exclamation and description.

We always have sin with us, but the sin of the problem of language is particularly destructive. Devaluation of language attacks the center of what it means to be human, and is devastating for culture. The same devaluation casts broadly based doubts on the primary means whereby God chooses to come to us, and is devastating for the church.

THE PURPOSE OF A
THEOLOGY OF LANGUAGE

The gospel comes to believers through Word and Sacrament. The gospel is a word of power which accomplishes that which it claims. Nevertheless, it is only the hearing of faith which knows the word of Jesus to be good news. God, through the Holy Spirit, quickens faith where and when God chooses. God decides when the word is to be written on the heart. If so, then one must ask about the pertinence of a theological discussion of language. Of course, the gospel of God will not be stopped by our misconceptions. Yet the word of the gospel, as with all words that are spoken, seeks a hearer, and that hearer's understanding of language can make a difference.

In the first place, a sound theology of language demonstrates the reasonable correlation between God's revelation as the word of Christ and our situation. Not everything in Christianity is unreasonable; it is really only God's sending God's only Son to die for us that is totally out of the ordinary. Christ's revelation in Word and Sacrament is in accord with his presence as urgent and personal, yet free and hidden. The spoken word and Jesus belong together. However, when the word of gospel becomes the word of Jesus "for you," it is always new and amazing.

In the second place, a sound understanding of the connection between the Word and words can keep Christians from certain fruitless practices. Much of the action of the church these days can be understood as an attempt to see God. Christians respond to their sense of the precarious nature of the church by building better programs, strengthening the budgets, and trying to increase membership. Not all of that is bad, of course, but much of it can be understood as an attempt to establish visual contact with the Creator. We should spend less effort trying to see God. God cannot be seen.

> Moses said, "I pray thee, show me thy glory." And he said, "I will make all my goodness pass before you, and will proclaim before you my name, 'The LORD'; and I will be gracious to whom I will be gracious, and will show mercy on whom I will show mercy. But," he said, "you cannot see my face; for man shall not see me and live." (Exod. 33:18-20)

God can be heard, and upon that hearing everything depends.

2
Words and the Word
in Our Culture

Straight got by heart that book to its last page:
  Learned, we found him.
Yea, but we found him bald too, eyes like lead,
  accents uncertain:
"Time to taste life," another would have said,
  "Up with the curtain!"

A Grammarian's Funeral, Robert Browning

Susan Langer has observed that the particular phenomenon which separates us from the animals is language. We are the animals who speak. Speech is the culmination of our bodily existence and the enactment of our spiritual dimension. Speech is bodily, issuing from the mouth to the ear. Speech is spiritual, exploding into meaning in an instant, then disappearing without letting us control or change it. Speech is also a part of the best of our mental work because thinking and language go together.

Some will answer that animals can speak too, and who would deny that animals have some rudimentary forms of communication? It can hardly be called language, however. In fact, our fascination with the primitive "speech" of animals is a sign of our deep sense that language is what separates us from them. I have a friend who is fascinated with the strange sounds made by whales, sounds that can be heard by other whales through hundreds of miles of water. There is usually someone who is fascinated with trying to teach apes to speak, knowing that if it can be done, there won't be anything to keep us from a very interesting visit. Even our old spaniel is a victim of this fascination. When we can get him to sit up and give a couple of little barks for a tidbit, he comes a little closer to being one of us. The unique miracle of human life is articulated when a child breathlessly tells of adventures at school, or a friend speaks of the prospect of a job, or one who has been offended says, "I was deeply hurt but please know that I forgive you."

Lately, "language" has been attributed to computers, and some of them have even been given hollow, disembodied human voices. Don't believe it! If animals can't speak, computers have even less capacity to do so. But to speak of computer "language" betrays our deep instincts again. We are in awe of the computer's capacity to do some of the things that we do, only faster and with greater accuracy. They are wondrous machines, and the highest accolade we can award is to give them speech. We are the animals who speak. It is our curse, but it is also our glory.

THE ROOTS OF LANGUAGE

Listening to the personal word of Jesus is at the heart of New Testament revelation. The gospels are, to be sure, filled with the commands of Jesus (Know ye! Believe! Come! Follow! Pray!). These commands give a certain tone to the gospels which can be interpreted as especially harsh and demanding, a plea for some sort of urgent action rather than for listening. Ernst Fuchs contends, however, that in many of the New Testament exhortations "a person is called upon to listen and is told he has to listen with regard to himself!"[1] These exhortations are not the heart of the gospel, and to listen doesn't guarantee that the gospel will be heard. But if Jesus is revealed, it will most often be in the telling of his story, in the speech which is in his name.

We have suggested that it is language which separates us from the animals. It remains to ask something about the nature and origin of human speech, not because a right understanding of language can bring God to us, but in order that we might understand that the avenues of revelation are still present and open. Knowing the roots of language cannot make us hear Jesus' voice, but it can teach us to listen. As is the case with all theology, it will not save us, but it can keep us from chasing down wrong and useless paths.

WHERE TO BEGIN?

Scholars have virtually given up on trying to determine just how language began. From the perspective of faith and biblical knowledge, speech is clearly a gift of God, a gift which is fundamentally related to the gift of breath and life. However, when scholars peer back into the dim beginnings of speech, they find so many mysteries that the search has virtually been abandoned. Those mysteries are all the more surprising when one realizes that studies of how contemporary children learn to speak abound. We may never know the precise answer as to how speech began, and certainly the best answer is the confession that language is a precious gift from the Creator.

Langer, upon whom much of this discussion depends, is convinced that scholars, in their search for the beginnings of speech, have been looking in the wrong places. Most investigators have assumed that language is a practical way of designating and reporting on those objects which fill our lives. For example, there are four-legged, domesticated animals that people have made pets. These animals are, for the most part, larger than cats and smaller than horses. They go about on all fours, lap water, and bark. It is expedient that we have a name for these creatures so that we can control and speak of them. We call them "dogs." (Notice, however, that we are not apt to call our own pet "dog," but rather a name.)

There are also certain flowers that are unlike any other. They are medium in size, thrive in cool but not freezing climates, and generally grow on bushes that have thorns. The flowers are various in color, and the bloom itself is very elaborately and delicately constructed. We designate them with the name "rose," and it does most often seem that they would smell as sweet by any other name. Are words simply designations, a way of organizing our experience of the objects out there? Could names, if we were able to remember them all, just as well be numbers?

If you give the matter some thought, it will soon become clear that there is more to speech and naming than designation. For example, the word *dog* also refers, in a general way, to certain lower forms of life or to a certain "dogged" persistence. To be a dog means to be subservient, and to be "dogged" means to be as persistent after some goal as dogs are after their basic needs. The word *dog* does much more than refer to another creature. It also makes real the relationship between speaker and creature and calls forth mutuality. Dogs can be persistent, and every pastor knows of parishioners who are not "dogged" enough in getting on with the ministry of the congregation. A rose can also be a color, someone's name, or a reference to a pleasant disposition.

Language is more than practical designation; a name is more than a number. Language emerges when we name the other; and in that naming, the presence of the other calls out to us. That other reality is already a reality in communion with the one who names, a reality which calls out to the other. Names, as well as language in general, do not just refer to that other, but enact or make possible the communion which waits to be realized. Our relationship to that other is also in the name. Roses could not be dogs, and dogs could not be roses. When those names are used, they not only refer to something, but a certain reality of meaning and relationship is brought into being. To have someone use our names too quickly, too casually, too often, is an invasion of privacy. It's no wonder that there is a definite sense of oppression when an aggressive salesman keeps prodding at you with your name. On the other hand, a name spoken at the right time, in love, marks the beginning of friendship.

SYMBOLS, ENVIRONMENT,
AND RITUAL

The origins of speech are not of interest for historians or anthropologists only, but for all Christians because we might gain some insight into how language works, particularly in our worship. Langer, in *Philosophy in a New Key*, makes a convincing argument for the following ingredients in speech formation: our symbolizing capacity, our childhood environment, and our tendency toward ritual.

A capacity for symbolization is at the root of speech formation, and all people have that in common. Apes can learn to make certain sounds to signify their desires or feelings. They can, for example, make sounds that indicate affection, but apes cannot name that sentiment. People are, by their very nature, symbol makers. "The earliest manifestation of any symbol making tendency, therefore, is likely to be a mere sense of significance attached to certain object, certain forms or sounds, a vague emotional arrest of the mind by something that is neither dangerous nor useful in reality. The beginning of symbolic transformation in the cortex must be elusive and disturbing experiences, perhaps thrilling, but very useless, and hard on the whole nervous system."[2] Apes may demonstrate some dim capacity for symbolization. They sometimes, for example, show an unusual and dramatic reaction to snakes. But people, who have the same basic aversion to snakes, are able to conceptualize their reaction (fear) and name the cause of it (snakes). People are even fascinated with the snake charmer who actually handles that evil reptile. Naming and speech emerge out of our uncanny sense of the presence, the reality, of the other.

The more immediate environment for the actual learning of speech has two primary ingredients: the infant's proclivity for babbling or lalling, and the matrix of mature conversation. Babies play with sounds; they simply enjoy making random noises with their mouths. Baby apes don't babble. Certain so-called "wild" children who have lived apart from humans cannot learn to talk even when surrounded by it. The lalling stage is crucial. Anyone who has learned a new language as an adult has some hint of that. The wonderful, happy babbling of a little one is the beginning of speech.

Nevertheless, speaking is not entirely a human instinct; that is, it is not produced in solitary by the lalling child. There must also be an environment of mature talk. Adults, who know the centrality of speech without thinking of it, will fuss mightily over whatever sounds a child makes. They might even imitate those childish sounds and become, thereby, a public embarrassment. But when a child says "ma ma," adults, particularly the mother, will become wildly enthusiastic. "The child's own mental activities are in some mysterious way engaged in and activated by this process, and before long he gradually forms the budding concept of mama or mother which goes with the spoken sound and applies this concept to the someone he has been coached into separating from the confusion and identifying as some sort of unified being."[3] To be sure, the mother was there before the child knew her name. The child saw her, touched her, and heard her. Is the name simply a designation for what she already was? If so, why does the mother get so excited? No, when the child says "ma ma," something new is added. This naming brings certainty, a conceptualized security, a blessed assurance, a vocalized praise which is at the very heart of what it means to be mother and child.

Speech may once have been song, although it certainly must very quickly have become what we know as speech. Otto Jesperson has shown how the voices of primitive peoples, particularly in passionate utterance, tend to fluctuate wildly.[4] Civilization, with its necessary suppression of passion, reduces the level of emotion in the voice. (It is no accident that cultured and educated people are often soft-spoken and that academic communities are ever so afraid of someone who "rants and raves.") Song does seem natural to us, a flowering of language if not its direct precursor. It is no accident that the singing of hymns has flourished in churches where preaching has been emphasized. Song and speech are closer than we might have realized.

Langer quotes from an article by J. Donovan wherein he places the roots of speech within the broader context of ritual.[5] We do know that people tend to attempt to recreate certain significant events in their history through pantomime and dance. Ritual recreation is common among all peoples but most obvious among primitive ones. Within the dance certain sounds are joined with symbolic gestures, and it might have been in ritual that those sounds became the first words. Articulate ritual would be more successful in calling the event back to mind and maintaining it in the consciousness of the dancers. Donovan contends that this means of holding onto the object by means of its symbol is so elementary that language has grown up on it. Ritual is basic to the lives of all of us, and has likely done more to establish community than we realize.

EMENDATION AND METAPHOR

One can imagine that the first language consisted of single-word sentences (words like *stop, really, eat,* or *beware*). The problem with one-word sentences is that they can too easily be misunderstood. Philip Wegner has recognized this and charts the development of more complicated speech along two lines: that of emendation and that of metaphor.[6]

Elemental speech, where it is misunderstood, demands some verbal creativity on the part of the speaker. Additional modifiers are needed to make the meaning specific and secure. Language grows through emendation, even to the point of the vast sentences of St. Paul. Specific modifiers are usually pulled into the vortex of a sentence by the force of its intent. Therefore, the key to understanding a sentence is most often to be found in the intent of the main message of that sentence rather than in the traditional uses of separate words.

If emendation is a creative act central to the development of language, Wegner contends that the making of metaphor is even more so. Where there is not an adequate way to speak of the impact, the novelty, the power which an event, thing, or person has upon the speaker, the speaker may resort to the powers of "logical analogy." Certain words, which actually speak of something else, are used to speak of the matter at hand. The hearer understands, for the context makes it clear that the language is not to be taken completely literally. "For instance, he might say of a fire: 'It flares up,' and be clearly understood to refer to the action of the fire. But if he says, 'The king's anger flares up,' we know from the context that 'flaring up' . . . is a symbol for what the king's anger is doing."[7] Here the context of what is said is appreciated for its typical importance, and the level of communion achieved through metaphor is higher than it could have been without it. Emendation and metaphor still conspire to make language the cradle of our life together.

One thing remains to this line of argument: it is a word of caution about how "symbol" is used. It is common for us to assume that symbol means the use of one thing to refer to another, that other being the thing that is meant. We tend to assume that all symbols are like the road sign which calls for caution because of the narrow bridge ahead. It points beyond to the bridge, but it is not yet the bridge. Does that mean that language, even at the point of its creative best as metaphor, is a sign or a reference pointing to something else? By no means. Speech as metaphor or symbol must be understood as being the thing itself for the auditor, an event in the world of sound. If the word came that the king's anger had flared up against you, you would already have reason to quake. Metaphor as symbol does not refer to distance or to a secondary reference, nor can one metaphor be easily substituted for another. Rather, metaphor simply provides that most immediate and typical element in our life of common speech.

PHILOSOPHY AND THOUGHTS
ABOUT SPEECH

Israel was not alone in its deep, intuitive appreciation of human speech. That was common among ancient peoples. The conception of language which is apparent in this prayer to Marduke was no different from that of Israel.

His word, which proceeds like a storm . . .
The word which destroys the heavens above
The word which shakes the earth beneath
The word is a rushing torrent against which there is no resistance
His word destroys the mother with child like a reed
The word of Marduke is a flood that breeches the dam
His word breaks off great mesu-trees
His word is a storm bringing everything to destruction
His word, when it goes about gently, destroys the land.[8]

What was unique to Israel was that a different God spoke to them, and that was and is a very great difference indeed.

Ancient peoples were simply not capable of the detached analysis of speech which makes it possible for us to say and believe that "talk is cheap." The ancients knew that talk can be cheap, but they also took it for granted that speech is the primary ingredient of our life together. As people who valued speech, they also knew how to listen—to listen for birds in the marsh, a footfall in the night, or the voice of God. They knew how to listen well, for once a sound goes unheard, it is gone forever. As Martin Buber has said, "We may state it thus, that the Jew of antiquity was more acoustically oriented than visually, and more temporarily oriented than spatially. Of all his senses he relied most heavily upon his hearing when forming a picture of the universe."[9]

Obviously, this concept of language is not our own. Routinely thinking so little of the value and meaning of speech is not only a sign of but a primary instrument in the decay of our culture. Fortunately, language still works, and the language of the gospel still sets the believer free. Nevertheless, it doesn't help to be in error; it sends us up blind alleys and down dark paths.

WERE THE GREEKS
THE CULPRITS?

Words are the instruments of philosophical investigation, and words bring us the past and create the future all at once. No wonder it is hard to know whether philosophy is descriptive or prescriptive. Even a cursory analysis of certain elements in the history of thought can give us some clues as to just how and why our appreciation of the spoken word has fallen to its present pass.

It was once fashionable for certain biblical scholars to assume that whereas Israel understood language to be constitutive of reality, the Greeks had it all wrong. Those scholars assumed that it was the Greeks who first began to teach us the lesson that words are merely pale shadows of those realities which were behind them. There is some truth in that contention, as we shall see, but it is very clear that many of the ancient Greeks knew and exercised the power of language from the same intuition and understanding as did the Hebrews.

The poems of Homer, which were the oral history of a people, reflect an orality which went up to and beyond the time of Plato. One can fairly hear these stories passed on from parent to child, from generation to generation. When someone recited oral history, it became present as one's own, giving knowledge, security, and identity. As a spoken story, it became the story of the speaker. There simply could not be the detachment that is possible with written history. Harold Strahmer points out that sometimes Homer's stories were recited from end to beginning, with the most recent events first. In speech, time cannot be altered and controlled as it can in writing. The speaker naturally thinks first of recent things. Aids to memory flourished in Homer's era, and young Greeks could learn Homer's poems with what would seem to us to be remarkable ease.

Whereas Homer's poems both represented and actualized a fundamental orality among the Greeks, there were individual thinkers who reflected on speech. Heraclitus was profoundly aware of the change, the flux, the movement which is the basic stuff of life. That change is both enacted and typified by the spoken word. Speech, however, enacts that change and flux which the speaker has in common with everyone. "Only in the mobile and multiform word, which seems to be constantly bursting its limits, does the fullness of the world-forming logos find its counterpart."[10]

Heraclitus also emphasized the conflict and polemic which is typical of life and which is explained as well as produced by orality. The point of view of the sophists of Plato's time was based upon their sharp sense of conflict and change. They were lecturers who went about speaking on such practical matters as public virtue, politics, and law. Sophists were very oral, emphasizing the persuasive power of speech as well as the art of rhetoric. The sophists were agreed that truth could be found through the give-and-take of conversation—the kind of exchange, for example, which is particularly present in a court of law.

People get nervous about the word *rhetoric*. Rhetoric suggests that too much of a claim is being made for the truth-bearing capacity of speech. People remember how speech can be used to fool and trick somebody, how it can mask and obscure what seems to be the truth. Plato got nervous about rhetoric too; and in his teaching on language one can see, clearly marked, the beginnings of a depreciation of speech which has been fulfilled in modern times.

Plato is anticipated by Socrates, who says of rhetoric that it is in the same class as cooking and refers to it as a "knack, a sham, a kind of flattery." Although Socrates was enough a part of oral culture to be reluctant to write anything, his dialogues do not seem to be a search for truth through discussion. Rather, Socrates knew the truth and uses dialogue to prepare his students to receive it. In the final section of the dialogue with Phaedrus, Socrates and Plato prove their oral roots by pointing out the inferiority of the written word when compared with the spoken. Nevertheless, for Plato language was too ordinary, too common, too concrete to be constitutive of reality. Speaking could only provide an image, a shadow of the reality which was beyond. In the tenth and last book of the *Republic*, Plato writes, "The great charge against poetry still remains. It has a terrible power to corrupt even the best characters, with very few exceptions."[11] Plato goes on to attack the Homeric tradition and ends up banning the poets from the Republic. Orality is suspect because of its ordinary, everyday capacity to deceive.

However different it may seem on the surface, our own disregard for orality, while more severe, has some affinity with Plato's suspicions. For Plato, language simply couldn't capture the idea or, if we take the roots of the word *idea* seriously, the "look of things." The subject-object split, which has been so deadly for speech, has not gotten us fully in its grasp until modern times. Nevertheless, its roots go back to before the time of Christ.

THE TRIVIUM:
THE REPOSITORY OF ORALITY

No clear line of demarcation can be drawn between an oral and a written culture, although it can be said that our modern conception and use of speech was given its shape by the Enlightenment. Even though Socrates had put rhetoric in the same category as cooking and other domestic chores, rhetoric survived until well into the seventeenth century. The primary elements in medieval education were grammar, rhetoric, and logic—the trivium. (A sign of how far we have come from that era is the difficulty that we have in thinking of medieval educators as teaching anything at all.) Grammar, although it had once referred to a general knowledge of certain writings, came to be identified with the process of writing. Rhetoric and dialectic, however, both maintained an emphasis upon orality.

Rhetoric was the study of the art of oral speech—the study of delivery and also, of more importance, the study of what goes into making a good speech. The orator was one who took a stand and wished to convince his hearers of his point of view. Rhetoric took the world of the hearer into consideration, that world which a good orator must understand. If we think of rhetoric as primarily ornamentation or verbal gymnastics, we are far from the truth; although, of course, speeches could become florid. Persuasion was the goal, and that end usually demanded a carefully crafted argument vis-à-vis the situation of the hearers.

Dialectic, with its roots in the give-and-take of conversation, also preserved a sense for the oral. To learn dialectic was to learn the art of argumentation. In order that the speaker's argument could anticipate objection and be convincing, dialectic concerned itself with the logical processes of the mind. Less attention was given to the total situation of speaker and auditor, more to the logic of human thought. Yet, as Walter Ong carefully points out, in the trivium, even though there was a concern for writing, the goal was not what we would think of as the objective facts. "Sweeping as it may sound, and even brash to say so, the fact is that from antiquity until well through the eighteenth century the formal education system that trained the western mind at no point undertook to train a student to be "objective." Objectivity could be

achieved and certainly was achieved, but its achievement was more or
less a matter of individual enterprise. What we today style objectivity
was not, indeed, positively downgraded. But in the academic world,
where the modes of expression taught were all rhetorical (persuasive)
or dialectical (disputatious), it was simply not provided for at all."[12]

Even though an understanding of speech as the bearer of truth continued in the educational system of the Middle Ages, the suspicion of
speech which we have seen in Plato was also active and growing. That
suspicion culminated in the Enlightenment, not because Platonic
thought was fulfilled, but because the Enlightenment offered a new
conception of reality. Our present cultural disparagement of speech is
rooted there.

THE ENLIGHTENMENT

Conflict, particularly in the form of war, was characteristic of the late
medieval period. Those wars can partly be understood in terms of the
antagonism and polemic which is typical of an oral society. Some scholars estimate that if the late medieval hostilities had continued, it would
have left Europe in a hopeless, indiscernible mess. The Enlightenment, with its emphasis on human reason and autonomy, was instru-
mental in putting life on a more even keel and in laying the groundwork
for modern democracy. Nevertheless, love of speech as the bearer of
truth was one of the casualties of the beginning of modern thought.

The thinkers of the Enlightenment did not teach the complete in-
dependence and the absolute private rights of the individual. They
were by no means the purveyors of everyone doing his or her own
thing. But they did teach that reality is held together by natural law,
a law which is present in the human mind and in the structure of the
world. To gain knowledge is to follow reason as we find it in ourselves.
Therefore, the self is the key to knowledge, and particularly the in-
quiring mind of the self. This conception of the search for truth served
to undermine the use of speech as the bearer of reality because it was
a solitary search, whereas speech is always reciprocal, communal. In
an oral culture, truth is the reality of the new life that springs up in
the give-and-take of everyday discourse; it is the product of the adventure of our life together. For the Enlightenment there was another
kind of truth, one sure and certain—a truth which was to be found

within. While the thinkers of the Enlightenment were not antagonistic toward language, speech became more a way of communicating truth already found than the vehicle of truth itself. Here were sown the seeds of our current pathological preoccupation with individual rights and individual freedom, although those seeds have only come to full flower in the recent past.

From the Enlightenment teaching that there is reason within and without, a reason available to private investigation, it is not far to the modern notion that truth is the objective reality "out there" which is mainly available to vision. The Enlightenment had emphasized the value of all the senses in the apprehension of reality, but seeing won the day. John Locke gave method to Descartes' call for private, isolated intellectual investigation. For Locke, the mind is like a dark room into which images of light come, a completely visualist conception of the sensorium. Reality consists of the objective facts that can be seen, touched, and measured. The way to truth is through experiment and investigation, and only when reality is already gained can it be expressed or signified by language. The culmination of this position, from the point of view of a philosophy of language, is positivism, where each word must be analyzed as to the verifiability of its object.

The investigative technique which is at the heart of science has given us much. The mere fact that children have a fair chance of growing into adulthood should keep us from being too critical. Yet there have been some great losses too—one of them being a sense for the lively, substantive exchange of human speech. Therapists are quite right to diagnose one of the great problems of our time as communication (it seems better to say "communion"), but they are not always aware of how deep-seated that problem is. The church has always been an oral community, for that is the nature of its constitution. Is it any wonder that it is struggling for its very life?

What has just been presented is nothing more than a bare outline of the way in which we have come to believe that "talk is cheap"; not that it might be cheap, for no one should deny that, but that it is cheap by its very nature. Lurking behind our conception of language is our fear of the fact that it can be cheap, that it is polemical, that it is naturally spontaneous and unpredictable. People always want to be certain, sure, positive. Although we may smile at the gospel singer's plea for "blessed assurance," it is what everyone wants. Speech is too communal, too ephemeral, too fleeting to be trusted. And who does not know that speech can do great harm? It can deceive, cajole, trick, flatter, hurt, insult, and boast. Words flung like arrows bring the deepest wounds. There is always some aggression in speech; it always lives just on the edge of chaos. Is it any wonder that we have tried to find truth elsewhere, in some more sure and certain way? "Talk is cheap, but seeing is believing."

Put this way, it is very clear that our denigration of speech is not only a mark of the decay of our culture but also the result of sin. Speech does not give us the kind of certainty we want, the assurance which we seek, an objective truth which we can use and keep. But our cure is worse than the disease. Ernst Cassier has written, "If we fail to find this approach—the approach through the medium of language rather than through the physical phenomenon—we miss the gateway to philosophy."[13] What is worse, we will miss the gateway to faith. Is it any wonder that the church is thrashing about, trying to outdo the world at what it does best? What else would one expect of a community which listens less intently for the voice from beyond, and that is more and more forgetting how to anticipate that story of Jesus which is both its charter and its mission?

WALTER ONG AND THE
STAGES OF THE WORD

The shape of the dilemma of the impotence of speech can be traced through the study of how language has been used. Walter Ong, a preeminent scholar of the history of the use of language, divides that history into what he calls "three stages of the word." Ong's stages cannot be clearly demarcated, for they tend to overlap by hundreds of years. The earliest stage, to some degree, still remains with us.

Before we can begin with stages, however, it is imperative to realize that "writing is derivative of speech, not vice versa."[14] Words were spoken before they were ever written down, spoken and then lost, carried away as though by the wind. Obviously, the spoken word came first, although it is difficult for us to imagine that it could ever have been so. "We are the most abject prisoners of the literate culture in which we have matured. Even with the greatest effort, contemporary man finds it exceedingly difficult, and in many cases quite impossible, to sense what the spoken word actually is. He feels it as a modification of something which normally is or ought to be written."[15]

Proof of Ong's point can be found in the teaching of language, which teaching we associate primarily with written rather than oral expression. Writing is a great blessing, a marvelous tool without which a complex society could scarcely survive. Mature citizens owe it to their neighbors to read and write with care. Nevertheless, there is a certain fundamental primacy in human speech which is somewhat lost in writing, a loss which is a part of our problem in speaking and hearing the gospel.

STAGE ONE:
ORAL CULTURE

Ong calls his first stage that of oral culture, or the unrecorded word. Language was spoken, and words were the crucial happenings of everyday life. Words did not merely designate reality but called reality into being. Certain aspects of orality remain in all of our lives, but we are so captive to written records that it requires an effort of the imagination to understand an oral stage in communication.

In oral culture, history took the form of the epic poem, a history which became an integral part of the one who heard and spoke it. Aids to memory flourished, and every good singer had certain patterns or themes that were used over and over again. (A few such devices remain: e.g., "Thirty days hath September, April, June, and November.") Long poems could be learned rapidly, but they were rarely done verbatim. In fact, it was common for a singer to wait for a few days to sing a poem which he had just learned. The song that eventuated was basically the same, although it was often slightly changed by the use of the singer's personal themes and memory devices. (The idea of verbatim correctness is a product of the age of print.) Through such singing history became contemporary, and the singer lived in both the past and present. Ong says that for the epic singer "the word is something that happens, an event in the world of sound through which the mind is enabled to relate actuality to itself."[16] Written history is something which one recalls from the past, whereas oral history, by its very nature, is a living part of the present.

Nowadays, in what is in certain respects an expanding typographic culture, "how to do it" manuals abound. The promise is that one can learn how to plumb a sink or bake a good cake by following written instructions. Such manuals did not exist in oral culture, where the learning of a trade depended on living as the apprentice of a particular tradesman. Anyone who has attempted to make or fix something "by the book" knows how awful it can be. Modern life is littered with the skinned knuckles, the broken appliances, the smoking automobiles, the torn stockings, and the picturesque language of those who have relied overmuch on manuals. In the vocal give-and-take between master and apprentice, a large number of eventualities could be anticipated. Not only is there greater flexibility in the apprentice method, it has the additional benefit of providing the learner with a model of solid work and business ethics. A good indication of how utterly captive we have become to the age of type is the naïveté that we have about the power and value of written instructions.

Oral culture had, and in its residual forms still does have, certain obvious benefits. Orality, above all, adds excitement and spontaneity to life, characteristics which a typographic culture trades for predictability and control. Nevertheless, one ought not be too romantic about orality, for it had certain limits which made it unsuitable for more advanced societies. Societies, like most organisms, become more complex as they live and grow. The history of a developed society becomes too vast for memory. Above all, extensive records must be kept. Studies show that the first impulse toward writing comes from the necessity of keeping records of business transactions; and scholars should not have been surprised, however disappointed, to find that most of the cuneiform tablets to be excavated have been records of bills. When a society reaches a certain level of self-consciousness and commerce, writing becomes a necessary vehicle for memory.

Certain themes and longer statements, mnemonically constructed for easier retention, were basic to oral culture. They were set statements about common subjects that the speaker had ready at hand. "Thus, to praise or vituperate an individual, one could proceed regularly through a sequence, praising or vituperating his family, descent, fatherland, sex, age, education, physical constitution, state of life, character, and occupation."[17] Gradually, as an oral culture moved toward becoming a typographic culture, some of the oral formulae were written down. In written form, as the "loci communes," various common, formerly oral, themes provided a main ingredient in medieval learning. However, what was held in common in orality became private and individual when communicated in print. Teachings became more public in print, with greater availability; but, at the same time, some of the personal, communal dimension of teaching and learning was lost.

STAGE TWO:
ALPHABET AND PRINT

Pictorial script formed a transition between orality and typography. Writing began with pictorial representation—very sophisticated examples of which remain, to take one instance, in Chinese characters. Such writing appears to have first been practiced among the Sumerians around 3500 B.C. and soon appeared in Egypt as well as the Indus Valley. Thus, writing developed rather late in the total history of humankind. Picture script was not far from the oral word, but it does mark the beginning of the process of getting speech into print and under control.

Before speech could be brought under more complete control, an alphabet was needed. An alphabet could not be fabricated or developed abstractly. It had to be discovered. That amazing event, one of the most significant in the history of Western civilization, occurred among north Semitic peoples sometime shortly before 1500 B.C. Every linear alphabet known is a descendant of that one.

The ability which the alphabet provided to fix the sound of speech in space, a dramatic change even over pictorial script, began a cultural revolution from which we have not yet recovered. Before print, words were sounds "going on," sounds which were crucial for life—listened for and let go as soon as they had been offered. In oral discourse there was at least some of the urgency that is present when a parent or grandparent speaks a few last words to the family. In writing, words escape the flow of time. Words are not so much events "going on" as records which are available. Ong has said, "The sense of order and control which the alphabet thus imposes is overwhelming."[18] Now records of debts could be kept, and contracts were written down. Now blessings could take legal form, and memory was replaced by visual aids. Now indictments could be widely circulated long after a hero had passed away.

The discovery of the alphabet, however, did not bring a quick end to oral culture. The old primacy of orality remained in various forms, all the way from Socrates' not writing anything down to the practice of reading aloud. (Augustine was surprised when he found Ambrose reading silently.) It was the invention of the printing press that gave the final and almost complete victory to typography over orality. Printing, as we know it in the West, began in Germany around the middle of the fifteenth century. The letter presses of the first German printers, which remained the most common method of printing until this century, made it possible to fix the spoken word in print with speed and accuracy. However, mass printing met with considerable suspicion. Jonathan Swift made fun of books, and even now authors complain endlessly about their publishers or are too scrupulous to commit ideas to the unforgiving immortality of print. Studies show that the capacity for mass printing was present long before people summoned the courage to use it. Perhaps they sensed that with the gain of print would come some loss.

Galloping individualism is both a characteristic and a curse of modern times. What greater disappointment is there for a modern person than the discovery that the promise of complete, personal freedom is a hoax! Many forces lie behind the growth of our preoccupation with private freedom, and an important one is the movement from oral to typographic culture. Seeing is something that one can and should do alone, whereas speaking and hearing is a communal event. Nowhere is that enforced isolation more tragically evident than in the life of the modern poet, the one who possesses language most intimately and gives it the greatest care. "By the nineteenth century, John Stuart Mill actually makes clear what is wrong, for he explicates the new mode of the existence of the poet, non-verbal and withdrawn, a 'loner'—quite the opposite of the gregarious oral bard."[19] Some poets know the present loneliness of language in their bones, and in their own sad and solitary lives.

The ear and the tongue are the primary organs of the human sensorium in an oral culture. In a world of speech and type, the emphasis is certainly on the eye. The eye is the chief instrument of scientific investigation, and we are convinced that "seeing is believing." A modern person intuitively believes that not having sight would be the worst thing that could happen to anyone, whereas studies show that children who cannot hear or speak, when left unattended, are more seriously impoverished than the blind. We are visual people, and that change in the sensorium means more than an alternative way of apprehending reality; it also marks a change in the way that the world seems to be.

To illustrate this change, Ong invites us to think about a medieval woodcut of a city, in particular a woodcut that can be shown to have represented several cities in the course of its visual life. Obviously the woodcut is meant to represent cities in general—what sort of sense of space one would have in a city and what the sounds of the market would be like. Someone with a strong oral bent might understand that at once. A visually oriented person, however, would most likely want to know just what particular city was the objective fact behind the woodcut. The chaos this creates for the Christian is obvious; we are endlessly trying to see rather than listen for God, and the Bible clearly states that God can never be seen.

STAGE THREE: THE ELECTRONIC WORD

Not long ago, my wife and I were shopping for a new radio. We found one that seemed about right, and I picked it from an open shelf to examine it more closely. Surely, if one is going to spend a significant amount of money on a radio, one ought to be able to examine the back as well as the front. In lifting it from the shelf, a burglar alarm was activated. A terrible squawking went through the whole store. People started hurrying toward me, and I must have looked just like a novice thief caught in the act. The department manager soon saw that the stuff of a major criminal is not in me. She explained that all the radios had to be wired that way because radios have become so popular that people are apt to carry them out without paying. The "Prairie Home Companion" by radio, phone calls by satellite, bills by computer, letters compliments of the word processor, and, of course, television, television, television. Ong is right. This is the electronic age.

What is amazing is that Ong is optimistic about the status of the oral word in our time. He is convinced that a resurgence in the understanding of the power of speech is upon us, and the amount of scholarship directly related to speech seems to confirm his judgment. How can this be? Ong articulates several reasons: one is our greater verbal mobility, and another is the breathtaking speed of computers.

The great mobility of our age makes it easier for people to talk to each other. Family visits, a main ingredient in the integrity of our life together, are still not as possible as in the days when parents stayed put and all the children settled nearby. Nevertheless, families can often get together now, at least in times of crisis; and when they do, they usually "just visit." People who do business together have greater occasion to talk; and just as despots have often gained authority through the evil use of speech, so also does constructive diplomacy depend upon visits between those who lead nations. Shuttle diplomacy is a good example of the orality made possible by our mobility. Letters have certain desirable characteristics, especially if one needs a permanent record or some time to think of a tactful way to say no, but there is no substitute for the mutuality of oral speech.

Ong believes that speech is emphasized, albeit in an oblique manner, by the computer. The speed with which a computer can print and disseminate information far outstrips the speed with which we can internalize it. "One of the troubles with electronic computers themselves is that often the printout is so vast that it is useless; there are not enough attendants to read more than a fraction of it."[20] Computer speed is breathtaking speed; and when that kind of mechanical haste comes near us, we are bound to long for the oral, the more digestible word.

Electronic media and the computer, however, also push us more directly in the direction of orality by giving us a sense of simultaneity. A typed record of events gives the reader a strong feeling of sequentiality and causality. Events march toward the reader out of the past, having been formed and shaped by their antecedents. Computers are so fast that they give the impression of simultaneity, a simultaneity not unlike that routinely produced by speaking and hearing. When a question is asked of a machine, the answer comes back as or more quickly than it would from a person. Modern methods have also made it possible to preserve the human voice itself. A taped, disembodied sound is not the same as the voice of living presence, but it gives a greater sense of immediacy than print. It's one thing to read those old Churchill speeches that some of us heard as children, but it's another to hear them. One is a history lesson; the other an occasion.

We are faced with a world which provides a bewildering array of stimuli for our senses. Computers, rock music, jet aircraft, on-the-spot reporting, blinking strobe lights, high-speed dental drills, and instant printing—can they be the matrix for a reevaluation of speech? Ong thinks so. Even if he is right, however, it will not and should not effect a romantic return to a more primitive age. We will not soon think of speaking and hearing in the way that the ancients did. Nevertheless, through reflection we can regain a greater facility for something that is primary in life. Christians may even stop trying to see God and start listening for that word which comes to us from beyond.

3
The Resources

Part 1—Theological: Luther and the Word

And though this world, with devils filled, should threaten to undo us;
We will not fear, for God has willed his truth to triumph through us;
The prince of darkness grim, we tremble not for him;
His rage we can endure, for lo! his doom is sure,
One little word shall fell him.

Ein' Feste Burg, Martin Luther

THE KEY TO LUTHER'S BREAKTHROUGH

Martin Luther broke through the medieval, Roman Catholic religious system. Modern Roman Catholic historians are quick to point out that the reform of the medieval church was much needed, although they disagree as to what form that renewal might have taken. Luther was by no means the first to see the ills of the church. Other reformers, both from within and without, had called the church to its knees, but none of them had broken through the vast system of theory and practice. Why was it that an obscure monk from an obscure monastery accomplished what others had not?

The time was right, say some. Luther would have agreed with that, for he considered the ills of the church against which he struggled to be genuine, robbing simple Christians of peace and hope. But the time had been right for a long time, and others had known it. Besides, to say that the time was right is a retrospective judgment more than a description of some aspect in Luther's consciousness. Others say that

47

Luther broke through the ancient and impenetrable system because of his unique combination of personal and intellectual powers. He was certainly able to grasp the key, the heart, of theological issues quickly. He could be charming and he was stubborn. Nevertheless, other reformers had been wise and possessed with a good measure of persistent cunning. To attribute Luther's breakthrough to his personal powers is to put the matter too simply. The typical Lutheran answer is that Luther discovered the gospel again and that it was the engine of the gospel that broke through the mighty wall of tradition.

That explanation comes very near the truth. Luther did not think of himself as having discovered anything new but as uncovering the gospel truth which had, for too long, been covered over. While "the gospel" is a correct answer as to why and how an obscure monk broke through the Roman system, it is a somewhat general answer. It would be more to the point to say that Luther came to understand anew that the gospel comes to us in language and to understand anew how that language works on the hearer. Luther found the theological key to unlock the great door of medieval Christianity, a key that Gerhard Ebeling has called "Luther's linguistic innovation."[1]

THE MANAGEMENT OF GRACE

The language of the gospel was the key to Luther's struggle from the very beginning. Paul Tillich has helpfully described medieval theology and practice as a "system of objective, quantitative, and relative relations between God and man for the sake of providing eternal happiness for man."[2] Grace was meted out to the common believer by the church, primarily through the means of the sacraments. It was done in such a way as to give the believer a sense of grace as an objective substance, something that one would do well to pile up a store of. (If the medieval Christian had been asked, in some antique version of our church questionnaires, whether grace was objective, that Christian would likely have said no. Believers knew that grace was not like a carrot or a potato. But psychologically, a sense of the objectivity of grace was inevitable.)

If grace seems to be objective, then it cannot very well be personal; it cannot be the living voice of Jesus. And if grace is objective, the believer is psychologically driven to store up a measure against that dark day which was never far away from the medieval person. Grace was not qualitative, like an embrace or loving word that changes things. It was more like banking spiritual certificates of deposit to be used when needed. That is what the indulgence practice was all about. Grace was relative, not absolute; there was never enough, so the conscience of many a medieval Christian was restless and without peace.

Behind this system was the persistent temptation for the medieval church to believe that God belongs to the church and that God's love can be managed. That same temptation stands at the door of every church building to this very day—the temptation to control the gospel. In the medieval church, the results of that temptation had been fixed in dogma and public teaching.

An objective, quantitative, and relative sense of grace was devastating for a person's conscience. Luther knew that very well, both from his own spiritual journey and from observing the Christians who lived around him. Luther knew that when a person can't get enough of the assurance which he or she needs to live, that person gets anxious. He also knew that anxiety was not what Jesus promised; it was not the "peace that passes all understanding." What set Luther on his road to reformation was his perception of the irony that the great medieval church system, which was ostensibly to bring people to certainty of their salvation, did just the opposite. Instead of blessed assurance, it meant an endless struggle to climb a ladder reaching toward a distant and holy God.

LUTHER'S ANSWER TO
THE MANAGEMENT OF GRACE

Just as the very practical problem of uneasy consciences started Luther on his struggle with the system that produced them, so also was his solution a very down-to-earth and practical one. Anxious people need the news of Jesus' love and forgiveness, and the preeminent way to receive that news is through the clear and simple speaking of the gospel. Luther's "linguistic innovation" was to disengage the gospel from the medieval machinery that controlled it and set it free by putting it on the lips of believers.

Luther knew that the freedom of God as spirit is truly honored when the gospel is conveyed in human speech. In the medieval system there was a sense of a certainty, a guarantee of grace, but always never enough. The spoken word has a certain freedom, a certain ambiguity at its center, but at the same time a certain completeness and finality, once it is heard, that is correlative with the gospel. When the gospel is spoken there is no guarantee that it will be heard as good news, or even that it is spoken out of a believing heart. It is up to God, in the freedom of the spirit, to bring the message home. Once heard as a personal word *pro me*, however, the gospel is enough. As Luther had learned so well from the baby Jesus—that which is common, ordinary, even despised, is often just the way that God comes to us. So it is with our ordinary words.

The word of the gospel is not the same as our everyday words, yet it is in our everyday words about Jesus that the gospel does come to us. Our faithful words, by the spirit of God, become words with the plus of revelation. Words are just the right vehicle, that vehicle which can and does become the very message of grace.

A PERSONAL, QUALITATIVE, AND ABSOLUTE WORD

The spoken word of the gospel is heard as a personal word. The spoken word of the lover to the beloved can never be an object to be kept and stored up, as a letter might be. It cannot be put off, diluted, or even interpreted. The spoken word is a personal word, just for the beloved, and it strikes to the heart. Hopes, dreams, fears, wounds, and ambitions are all touched by the personal word of the gospel. The gospel makes Jesus' story our story.

The spoken word of the gospel is heard as a qualitative word, not a quantitative one. The word of love from lover to the believing beloved is not about some aspect of life outside the lover or some condition that will apply when requirements are met. No, it is the very heart of the lover that is revealed in that very moment. The lover's word is not a word about love; it is love.

The spoken word of the gospel is heard as an absolute word, not as a relative or conditional word. When the lover speaks a word of love to the beloved it is, just then, sufficient. The quality of life is changed.

Soon, of course, that word of love may be heard again, but always as a new and free word, not as a word in a sequence being stored up.

Luther believed, and so must we, that the Word of God is infinitely more than information about what God is like. The gospel is a word that changes a believing person. Christians are changed when the Word of God is written, by the spirit, on the heart. By virtue of the inescapable dominion that people have over the creation, it is also a word that changes life at the broadest levels of society. The writing of the spirit on the heart can certainly come through reading print, but the preeminent word which leads to faith is the lively, living word of human speech.

Christian life can be understood, at one level, in terms of a person's visible actions. Luther wanted to take the issue a step further and ask just what it is that calls a person into action, just what it is that summons us to be what we are. Certainly we are what we are because of the action of all of our senses, but the way that we are called forth by listening to different "drummers" is characteristic of life at its deepest level. For example, one's vocation, if it is truly a work which is treasured, is most accurately described as a calling. People most content with their labor often have a distinct sense of having been summoned into it. Left to our own ambitions and passions, life would be a solitary dance toward death. We would be alone. Rather, people live best by responding to the voices from beyond, and one of those voices is that of our Lord Jesus. When his voice calls us into being, our word, as well as the rest of our actions, is truly in behalf of the neighbor.

Luther's conception of theology as a linguistic innovation demands just as much precision of thought as does the most complex, speculative scheme. It is not easy to figure out just what voices and forces in life call us toward anxiety and fear and away from faith and love. It is not easy to figure out just how life and language are in accord with the spirit of the risen Christ. It is not easy to keep from looking into the heavens for the signs of God, when all the while the incarnate One is present in the weak but faithful murmurings of our neighbor. Above all, it is not easy to remember that we are by no means saved by our theology, which can only keep us from chasing down wrong paths, but by the spirit-given revelation of God.

THE SPIRIT AND THE LETTER

Such is the confidence that we have through Christ toward God. Not that
we are competent of ourselves to claim anything as coming from us; our
competence is from God, who has made us competent to be ministers of
a new covenant, not in a written code but in the Spirit; for the written
code kills, but the Spirit gives life. (2 Cor. 3:4-6)

Luther's theology is systematic in the sense that it has a sure and
certain center from which all aspects of Christian life can be understood. One will not find a series of nicely ordered propositions, but
something like a circle at the center of which is Luther's conviction
that we are justified by faith apart from works of the law. At the center
of his "system" is his conviction about the nature of the gospel as an
utterly free and saving event. Whatever theological point Luther argued, whatever counsel he gave, whatever sermons he preached, it all
led to the one, central matter.

One of the perspectives which gives us a good look into the heart
of Luther's theology, and thereby gives us a vision of the whole, is the
vantage point of 2 Cor. 3:6. For our purpose of trying to understand
Luther's theology of the word, especially as it applies to the spoken
word, there is no more important verse. For Luther, the word of the
spirit is preeminently the spoken word of faith.

Luther's treatment of 2 Cor. 3:6 is nowhere clearer than in his attack
on one of his theological enemies, Jerome Emser. The debate between
Luther and Emser began in 1519 when Emser published an open letter
offering assurances that Luther's position at the Leipzig debate had not
been too radical and was not linked with the more serious errors of
the Hussites. Luther smelled something fishy in Emser's supposed
conciliation. It seemed to him that Emser was actually trying to take
some of the bite from his words at Leipzig. One thing led to another,
and before long, Luther and Emser were at each other's theological
throats.

At issue was the authority of the church to interpret Scripture, in
particular 1 Pet. 2:9, "You are . . . a royal priesthood." Luther was
convinced that this passage, taken in its plain meaning, meant that all
believers are priests, one to the other. Emser, out of his conviction
that ecclesiastical authority can override the simple meaning of the

text, fought for the superiority of the priestly estate. Their battle culminated in 1521 when Luther wrote his "Answer to the Hyperchristian, Hyperspiritual, and Hyperlearned Book by Goat Emser in Leipzig— Including Some Thoughts Regarding His Companion, the Fool Murner."[3] In his treatise, Luther makes considerable use of 2 Cor. 3:6 in order to bring light upon the issue of how "You are a royal priesthood" should be interpreted.

When Emser was forced to interpret the words "the letter kills but the Spirit gives life," he did so in terms of two meanings in Scripture, one external and one hidden, one literal and the other spiritual. Luther writes, "The literal meaning is supposed to kill, the spiritual one is supposed to give life. He builds here upon Origen, Dionysius, and a few others who taught the same thing. He thinks he has hit the mark and need not look at clear Scripture because he has human teaching. He would also like me to follow him to let Scripture go and take up human teaching. This I refuse to do, even though I too have made the same error."[4] For Luther, the obvious and immediate problem with stating the twofold meaning in that particular way was that it gave ecclesiastical authorities too much freedom of interpretation. The church gained license to use the spiritual meaning to justify its own practice, and the prophetic power of Scripture, as over against the church, was lost.

Luther's criticism of Emser was rooted in two aspects of his passion for oral language. The product of the letter of Scripture is to be the word of the gospel, which is, preeminently, the spoken word of Christian witness. But Luther's interpretation of texts grew out of his idea of the power of orality, too. Interpreters have always known that the plain letter will not suffice. There must be something more. For Emser, that "extra" was the spiritual meaning, whereas for most modern interpreters, it is the history or the meaning behind the letter of the text. Luther's deep appreciation for the living character of language, especially in its oral form, made it possible for him to take the text seriously as it stands, as a lively and engaging gospel word. His question of the text was not, What actually happened? or, What does this mean? but, What are these words clearly saying to us?

Luther also attacked Emser's particular version of the distinction between letter and spirit by reflecting on the metaphorical capacity which is natural to language. "For example, if I said, 'Emser is a crude ass,' and a simple man following the words understood Emser to be a real ass with long ears and four feet, he would be deceived by the letter, since through such veiled words I wanted to indicate that he had a crude and unreasonable mind."[5] Luther points out that Scripture is full of such figures. He offers, among others, the example of how Christ calls Christians the salt of the earth and the light of the world. In commenting on the salt and light passage, Luther drove hard toward his own interpretation of the distinction between spirit and letter. The words *salt* and *light* have to be taken absolutely seriously, in their most earthy sense. Yet the very fact that Christ says "you" are the salt and the light shows that a more spiritual meaning might accrue. That spiritual meaning, for Luther, had nothing to do with a special language being used within the reference of a sophisticated system of interpretation. The spiritual meaning could never be separate from the literal but had to arise from a real knowledge of salt and light. Thus, the gospel meaning depends on the simple, clear word of Scripture being brought to bear on the hearer in the hope that it might be a word enlivened and written on the heart by the spirit. That bringing-to-bear for the hearer is best done through the spoken word.

In arguing for a "grammatical, historical meaning" of Scripture, Luther writes, "It would be appropriate to call it the meaning of a tongue or a language, as St. Paul does in 1 Cor. 14:2–19, because, according to the sound of the tongue or speech, it is understood in this way by everyone."[6] Luther's distinction between letter and spirit was a distinction made without separating the two—a distinction made because he understood how the language of the gospel worked, and because he left room for the blowing of the spirit by giving priority to human speech for the gospel's enactment.

"You are the salt of the earth and the light of the world" is most personally and powerfully brought to bear on another through the spoken word. There is freedom in the metaphorical usage, but that is not yet the freedom of the spirit. The simple hearer is readily able to think most concretely about "salt" and "light," about how salt cauterizes and preserves, and about how even a small light gives uncanny illumination to dark places. It is impossible to take the letter too seriously. Yet, the letter is not the spirit, for the spirit is most clearly involved with the little word *you*. Clearly, the word *you* in the sentence refers to a certain status that the hearer has, and a certain posture toward life as well. But that "you" is not always heard, for with the "you" one is dealing with matters of the heart; and if it is heard, it may not be accepted. If the statement which, from the viewpoint of God, is already true, is heard by the heart of faith, then it becomes true for the hearer. It is the gospel. The letter is not gone; salt is still salt and light is still light; but now they have been written on the believer's heart.

In language, better than any other way, Jesus comes into the world as one who is utterly near and yet hidden. It ought not amaze us so much that Jesus comes to us in the spoken word, but rather that it is Jesus who comes. When the announcement of the gospel, which has its literal and earthly frame of reference at the cross, becomes a saving word for you or for me, it is the work of the spirit. Understood in this way, as Gerhard Ebeling has rightly observed, the world of the spirit is simply the world of faith, of true understanding. The letter of the spoken word of the gospel is like the letter of any language, except that this time the letter embodies a certain Jesus who went down to death between two thieves. The freedom of the language of the gospel is congenial with the spirit, for it is within that realm of language, as well as in the realm of the letter, that the spirit of God is at work.

LAW AND GOSPEL

Luther's teaching about law and gospel is also best understood in terms of the relationship between faith and language. Robert Jenson writes, "This dogma is not a particular proposed content of the church's proclamation, along with other contents. It is rather a meta-linguistic stipulation of what kind of talking—about whatever contents—can properly be proclamation and word of the church."[7] Law and gospel is a way of describing what the language of justification is like; either it is a word that tears down and convicts or it is a word that saves and sets free. If the preached word is a word in between law and gospel, and the two are absolutely separate extremes between which there is ample room to fall, it is not the word of Christ. When Christ speaks the word of his claim on us, there is no neutral ground.

Just as the spoken word is living, immediate, and passing away, so also the distinction between law and gospel is a distinction that the preacher must always be making. It is not one dogmatic formula among others that can be learned once and for all, but a distinction made on the move. A person can become adept at making the law–gospel distinction, and Luther calls that aptitude the work of a true theologian, but it cannot ever be mastered. As a distinction made on the move, it is like learning to pass in an automobile. Passing demands the making of distinctions "en route"; and while one may become good at passing, who would ever be foolish enough to say that it had been mastered!

Just as work with language is called a craft or an art, the preacher who distinguishes between law and gospel has a certain facility, what Jenson calls a "knack." That knack, at the most elementary level, is to remember that the letter of the law must be spoken, and to arrange speech so that the law stands clear and is not diluted. More difficult is the knack for heading off the hearer's escape from the word of the gospel. Luther knew very well that people will flee from the gospel, that they will return again and again to their old haunts of the law, even though it means death. " 'Rightly dividing' the law and the gospel is the knack of so making promises in Jesus' name as endlessly to transcend this turn back to the law." It is like keeping a crazed animal from plunging back into a burning barn.

When Luther wrote that the prince of darkness could be completely undone by "one little word," he meant one little word of the gospel. So confident was Luther of this point that he insisted that where the word of the gospel was truly spoken, there Christ was truly present. For Luther, the gospel word does not signify Christ, but it is really Christ. As Bonhoeffer so beautifully puts it, the gospel word becomes "Christ walking through the congregation as the word."[9] Our rather wide-ranging theological speculation as to whether the finite can contain the infinite is more productive when narrowed to the question of whether someone can truly be present in his or her words. Our answer is yes, fully and completely. The wonder of Christ's real presence in his word is that it is the suffering, dying, forgiving Jesus who is with us, the risen One whose body is the church.

Part 2—Biblical: Words and the Word in the Bible

For as the rain and the snow come down from heaven,
and return not thither but water the earth,
making it bring forth and sprout,
giving seed to the sower and bread to the eater,
so shall my word be that goes forth from my mouth;
it shall not return to me empty,
but it shall accomplish that which I purpose,
and prosper in the thing for which I sent it. (Isa. 55:10-11)

We have seen that one of the marks of our culture is a serious depreciation of the spoken word, so much so that it is difficult to think of speech as a way in which the gospel of Christ can be actualized. If talk by its very nature is cheap, how can we expect much of the language of the church? Parishioners often assume that the sermon, as an act of language, cannot have much power. What is worse, many pastors assume the same thing. Sermons are by no means the only aspect of our worship and life together which suffers. A toll is also taken of the sacraments and of conversations between believers.

The purpose of this chapter is to demonstrate that it has not always been so. Rather, in Scripture itself, that book which is the guide and norm for our teaching and life, language is given a crucial place. We shall attempt to show that the spoken word is the bedrock upon which the edifice of the Scriptures is built. To be sure, there are deeds in Scripture other than spoken ones aplenty, but it is important that Jesus himself is finally called the Word, that word which proceeds out of silence to give life and hope.

The point of knowing about the oral roots of Scripture is not to coax us to understand the world in the same way that the biblical figures did. To retreat into another way of thinking is impossible. But, in spite of our prejudice against the spoken word as a vehicle of power, we can at least learn to expect our Lord Jesus to draw very near to us, as near as human speech. We can at least learn to expect more of the language of our worship. We can at least learn to proceed to the craft of proclamation with imagination and dedication. That would be very good for speaker and listener alike.

THE BIBLE:
SPEAKING FIXED IN PRINT

Our experience of the Bible is primarily that of a written book, of words fixed in print. We like it that way, for words that we can see and a book that we can handle give the message of the Bible a certain permanence, the feel of truth. Words, in our era, become true when they are written down, signed, sealed, and delivered. Our experience of the Bible as a written book may be greater than ever before. Children are not so apt to be required to learn and repeat portions of the Bible orally; and when texts are read in worship, we are becoming more and more accustomed to reading along.

Nevertheless, most of the Bible was born in speech and not in writing; it was an "oral" book before it became a written one. It is easy to imagine how some of the stories of Israel's patriarchs and heroes were once passed on by word of mouth. The psalms were sung in worship; and the prophetic books, for the most part, contain a portion of the preaching of Israel's prophets. A chief characteristic of Israel's poetry is parallelism, reflective of the repetition which is the punctuation of oral discourse. The Old Testament is also full of alliteration, onomatopoeia, and paranomasia, all of which reflect the linguistic play characteristic of orality. We don't really know that Jesus wrote anything; but his speaking, as well as other actions, proved to be unforgettable, and later came to be written down in our Gospels. Paul's letters were written to churches that he had established with his preaching, and only as a concession to not being present. No one ever sat down to write the Bible, at least not in the same way that an author sits down to write a novel. The Bible was born in speech, in the faithful conversation between Israel and her God and between Jesus and his followers.

It seems a little frightening to think that much of the Bible was born out of the spoken word. That knowledge threatens to take away the Bible's truth, its authority, its power. That knowledge threatens to rob us of one last thing to hold onto, one last assurance. But God wishes to speak a contemporary word to us, a word out of God's revelation in the past but a word as near to us as our own hearing. When a living word of Scripture comes to us, we cannot avoid or control it. God's

word breaks in on us as the saving voice of Jesus—challenging, de-
stroying, loving, giving hope. After all, letters from a dear one are fine,
but there is no substitute for the living voice.

THE CREATION:
GOD SPEAKS AND IT IS SO

And God said, "Let there be light"; and there was light.

And God said, "Let there be a firmament in the midst of the waters, and
let it separate the waters from the waters."

And God said, "Let the waters under the heavens be gathered together
into one place, and let the dry land appear." And it was so.

And God said, "Let the earth put forth vegetation, plants yielding seed,
and fruit trees bearing fruit in which is their seed, each according to
its kind, upon the earth." And it was so.

And God said, "Let there be lights in the firmament of the heavens to
separate the day from the night."

And God said, "Let the waters bring forth swarms of living creatures, and
let birds fly above the earth across the firmament of the heavens."

And God said, "Let the earth bring forth living creatures according to
their kinds: cattle and creeping things and beasts of the earth according
to their kinds." And it was so.

(Gen. 1:3, 6, 9, 11, 14a, 20, 24)

When Christians think of God the creator, they may imagine just
how it was that God actually went about creating. Perhaps the most
common, most childlike idea is that God made things with great hands,
like our own only much larger. In Genesis 2, it does seem that God
formed man and woman in that way. A handmade creation is a childlike
idea, however, for we know that God is spirit and may not always do
things the way that we do them. Could it be that a more mature
assumption would be to simply assume that God has been and is the
creator, without having any notion of just how that works? Yet, a distant,
abstract creator wouldn't be much of a personal comfort and would
certainly have to fall behind the movement of history. There is a certain
childlikeness that we cannot escape. Could it be that God actually does
create with those great hands?

Perhaps so, but the creation account at the very beginning of Genesis
conveys another impression. God speaks, and in speaking brings forth
the creation. In the poetic, busy, driving account of creation in Gen.

1:1—2:3 it is God's voice which brings the new into being, which gives form to the formless and shape to the shapeless. God said, "Let there be . . . ," and heaven and earth came into being. God spoke again to make plants grow on the earth, lights shine in the heavens, and creatures swarm in air and sea. The ritual of simple utterance and subsequent formation was not quite the same when God created people. Nevertheless, the entire act was characterized by the speech of God— the announcement of the intent to create people, the injunction to be fruitful and multiply, and the call to have dominion over the rest of the creation. Clearly, God did not create with great hands but with a word, a spoken word which summoned the creation into being. God spoke and it was so.

The creation account says something about God but also teaches us that the spoken word is vital to our understanding of who God is and to our understanding of ourselves as God's creatures. If there is unique, creative power in the speech of God, so also unique power and responsibility are given to those members of the creation who are given the gift of speech. It is primarily in speaking that we have our dominion over the creation. In the creation account which begins with Gen. 2:4, the gift of speech is tied directly to the uniqueness and responsibility of people. God brings in the creation of people by forming a person from the dust. But before long people spoke, and it is in their speaking that the secret of dominion is revealed.

Birds of the air and beasts of the field are brought to the man that he might give them names. Naming gives us a hint of what is uniquely human, and also a hint about what it means to have dominion. People are the ones who can speak, who can name the birds and the beasts. None of the other creatures can do that. When names are given to the creatures, it is not just that they are being designated for what they already are. Rather, in the naming they become what they are; their nature and character are called forth. Amos Wilder writes, "Social psychologists tell us that the birth of language and myth is simultaneous with world-making. The primitive does not first see an object and then give it a name. Rather in naming it he calls it into being."[10] Not that a toad wouldn't be as squat by another name, or a giraffe as tall. Rather, in the naming of a bird or animal, a certain category is given, a certain identity drawn out, a certain responsibility taken by the one who names.

Even as God is able to bring reality into being with speech, so also are people given a share of that creative power. Speech is the mark of our dominion. Dominion is not something that we may choose or reject, although it is certainly something that we may abuse. Dominion is simply something that we have been given, a status marked and actualized by our ability to speak.

> Let all the earth fear the LORD,
>   let all the inhabitants of the world stand in awe of him!
> For he spoke, and it came to be;
>   he commanded, and it stood forth. (Ps. 33:8–9)

Certain psalms also describe the close relationship between the formative power of God's word and the creation. In Psalm 33, the Lord flings out the heavens with a word and brings out their host with a breath. The children of Israel are to worship God in fear and awe exactly because the heavens stood forth when God commanded them to. One might well be in awe of someone whose voice strikes down or builds up with such alacrity.

Yet the creative word of the Lord is not fickle or capricious, but an upright word which is faithful to the purposes of God's love. When God calls someone or something into being, that creation is no shadow or distorted image of what it might be, but it stands in harmony with the rest of the creation. The creation is beautiful and perfect because what God calls into being *belongs.* Anyone who has looked into the night sky knows that the heavens and their host belong together. God would not have thought to create them any other way.

> The heavens are telling the glory of God;
>   and the firmament proclaims his handiwork.
> Day to day pours forth speech,
>   and night to night declares knowledge.
> There is no speech, nor are there words;
>   their voice is not heard;
> yet their voice goes out through all the earth. (Ps. 19:1–4a)

Psalm 19 represents a vivid statement of how the creation responded to having been created. The heavens themselves "tell the glory of God" and the "firmament proclaims his handiwork." Day after day the elemental parts of the universe pour out their praise to the creator. To be sure, the heavens do not have speech as we have it, yet their voice goes out through all the earth. When the heavens gave praise to God, it had to be in the form of sound, of speech or song. How else can anyone or anything properly thank a God who creates with a word!

For years Christians spoke and sang of the "music of the spheres," those ethereal anthems sent up by the heavenly bodies in praise of their creator. Now the universe is often thought of as utterly silent, a deadly cold and alien world, divorced from us as an austere citadel of lifelessness. One cannot help but wonder if the universe has stopped its singing, or is it that we no longer know how to hear its song? Yet, in a meadow outside Cambridge, England, a long row of radio telescopes, like so many metal ears, listen day and night for the sound of the universe.

The conviction that God continues to create is both a necessity and a blessing for faith. But belief in the present creative power of God has never been easy to sustain. When theologians of our modern era began to think in terms of mechanical causality as the life force of history, the logical alternative was to believe that God once created everything but is no longer involved in the ebb and flow of life. The God of the Deists started the world up but then stepped aside to let it run along on its own course. Deism has been rejected by twentieth-century theology, but it is still very much a part of Christian thinking. If the present is born out of the womb of its own causality, how can we understand God's creative power in our world?

If God once created with a word, it is reasonable to assume that it is still so. Of course, there are certain basic forms of life that seem to grow simply, causally from their antecedents. Yet even these forms must be named. Much of what is truly new in life is called forth by, marked with, and remembered in the everyday conversation of all peoples. And for the Christian, it is still a life-giving word of God in Jesus that breaks into our world to create faith. God once created with a word, and it is still so.

THE PROPHETS:
GOD ACTING IN WORDS

Then Amaziah the priest of Bethel sent to Jeroboam king of Israel, saying, "Amos has conspired against you in the midst of the house of Israel; the land is not able to bear all his words." (Amos 7:10)

The anger of the priest Amaziah against the prophet Amos should not surprise us. Amaziah was in charge of King Jeroboam's sanctuary and could be expected to be fully in support of that regime. When Amos announced that Jeroboam would die by the sword and the people go into exile, Amaziah knew that his livelihood was in danger. That is not surprising. What is unusual is the language that the priest uses to describe the word of Amos: "The land is not able to bear all his words." The words of the prophet are heavy, full of foreboding, threatening of life. They are as real and as powerful as rocks. God's words changed the lives of hearers in the same way that a fallen meteorite might change the surface of the earth.

When a child first becomes acquainted with the Bible, a common reaction is surprise over the way in which the word of God comes out of the mouths of prophets. How can that divine word come out of the mouth of a mere mortal? Sometimes it is hard to tell if it is God or the prophet who is speaking. How can this be? It is, of course, because God has chosen to come to people in speech, that element of life which binds us most surely in common. It was not so amazing to Israel that God should come to them in the words of the prophets, but what was amazing was the arresting, condemning, life-giving character of the words themselves. To hear God's word was to come face to face with God. One can find in the prophets, perhaps better than anywhere else in the Old Testament, a faithful conception of the vitality of speech which we have virtually lost.

Gerhard von Rad has called the prophets' conception of language "dynamistic."[11] The prophets did not reflect much on what language meant to them; but from this distance, across great changes, we can say that their understanding of language was "dynamistic." For the prophets, language did not convey an idea from the mind of the speaker to the mind of the hearer; rather, the word was almost material, concrete, an event itself. Just as all language conveys the actual person of the speaker, so also the word of the prophet was the real presence of the person of God. Thus, when God spoke by the prophet, that word did not express the sentiment or opinion of God; that word was God acting within history.

Because there has been an evolution in our thinking about and use of speech, it is very difficult for us to understand even the prophetic words as actions. But von Rad is by no means willing to conclude that this prophetic, dynamistic use of language is utterly lost. He will not settle for leaving that "magic" in the past. The prophets reflect something which is still basic and fundamental to a faithful hearing and use of all human speech, particularly if it becomes the speech of God.

One of the most eloquent statements of the power of God in the mouth of the prophet is found in Isa. 55:10–11. How vivid and everyday the material of the language is: the rain and snow which water the earth, and the seed which makes bread for the eater. The naive and yet profound understanding of nature behind these words is the simple realization that when moisture falls to the earth, it does not return to the atmosphere without having done something. Rain naturally gives growth to the grain. So also the prophetic Word of God is a word which does and will do what it says. The full accomplishment may take some time, but once that word is spoken, it is already working in the world to fulfill its linguistic destiny.

Here it must be emphatically stated that the Word of God, however human in the mouth of the prophet, was by no means thought of as another mortal word. Our words are never complete, never just right; but God's word is called "the" word because it is always just the right word for the particular situation of the believer. It may be a difficult and challenging word of judgment or a life-giving word of blessing; but God's word, even if it doesn't seem so, is always the word that we need to hear just then. The prophets did not arrive at any "theory" of language primarily by observing prophets' ways, but they were in faithful communion with God and sensed the wonder of all language in God's words. The Word of God is the word of the prophet; yet it is not another mortal word. This is a mystery, a wonder not unlike that greater mystery of Jesus' being the carpenter's son from Nazareth and also God with us.

The prophets Jeremiah and Ezekiel depended so much on the words of God that they ate them. In Jer. 15:10–21 the prophet made a great and personal lament over his situation. God had given him words to speak, and he had taken those words into himself. Jeremiah had eaten them and found delight in their flavor. But then, as the spokesman for God, he suffered the unrest that is often stirred up by the divine word. Jeremiah was cursed by his hearers, and they plotted vengeance against him. His "pain was unceasing" and his "wound incurable." The prophetic word was doing its work all right, but it was a work of judgment and not of blessing. The prophet complained, but God did not exactly promise to spare Jeremiah, who was to continue to be the mouth of God. The best that could be said is that God would sustain him in his lonely duty and vindicate the word which he spoke. Jeremiah was still to be sustained by the difficult word; it would be as precious to him as bread to the eater.

Ezekiel ate the scroll of the word of God when he was commissioned to be a prophet (Ezek. 2:8–10). Those words, once eaten, had to be spoken to his own people—words of lamentation, mourning, and woe. Such words were bound to make the prophet's life difficult because the people "will not listen to him," and here "not listening" refers to a rebellious and angry hearing. The word was "like flint" to the hearers, a word of judgment doing its work, setting Ezekiel apart. To add to Ezekiel's burden, he had to proclaim the words of God knowing very well that they wouldn't be heard. Nevertheless, that word was "as sweet as honey" in Ezekiel's mouth, a word which sustains him as does food.

To consider these prophetic "eatings" primitive and crude is to say more of us than it does of the prophets. How can anyone live without the good of the language of everyday community, and what preacher doesn't know something of the combined blessing and burden of a word within, waiting to be spoken? We need food to live; and in the same way, for we cannot live apart from the word, we need the speech of God.

JESUS:
THE WORD MADE FLESH

When Jesus is identified as the Word of God, the development of the centrality of speech in the story of God's revelation is made complete (1 John 1:1–4; John 1:1–18; Rev. 19:13). Just as Jesus is given personal titles such as "son," so also is he called "the word." The coming of the Word marks a new and dramatic episode in the history of salvation, the time of the inbreaking of God's personal and final word to God's children. The one who spoke and called the creation forth now speaks in and through Jesus, and through the words of Jesus new life is created.

> That which we have seen and heard we proclaim also to you, so that you may have fellowship with us; and our fellowship is with the Father and with his Son Jesus Christ. (1 John 1:3)

In the opening verses of 1 John, Christians are reminded that the revelation of God in Jesus is visual and tactile as well as oral (1 John 1:1–4). The life of the revealer was a public life, and part of the social reason for crucifixion was that it be a visual warning to all who passed by. People also touched Jesus, and when he came as the risen one, the disciples had to get their hands on Jesus to make sure. Christians of every age seek assurance, and the best certainty available often appears to be tactile or visual. Certainly our visual surroundings in worship are important, and we do feel the elements of the sacraments on the head, in the mouth, and on the hand. Nevertheless, that writer of 1 John cannot avoid the preeminently spoken character of the gospel who is Jesus. That which was from the beginning, the word of life, is *heard.* Now the only thing for the Christian to do is to proclaim that life which has been made manifest, so that fellowship might abound with joy.

> In the beginning was the Word, and the Word was with God, and the Word was God. (John 1:1)

> And the Word became flesh and dwelt among us, full of grace and truth; we have beheld his glory, glory as of the only Son from the Father. (John 1:14)

The little prologue to 1 John is clearly correlative with the mighty prologue to the Fourth Gospel. John, in his great theological preamble (John 1:1–18), makes the most substantive identification of Jesus as the Word in the entire Bible. A reading of those difficult and complex opening verses will give the reader an unmistakable sense that "word" here is no longer a simple designation for human speech. The.word which is now Jesus is a word which has been with God from the very beginning, a word that dwells among us, full of grace and truth. John the Baptist bore witness to this one who is the word, but John was not the word. Jesus, as the Word, ranks before John. John's prologue is heavy going. The "word" doesn't seem as clear and obvious as simple speech between friends.

Sometimes specific words become necessarily complex and many-sided over the passage of time. Such is the case with the *logos* of this prologue. For the Stoics, "word" meant reason or wisdom, that material or idea which energized and sustained the world. John might have been affected by their thinking and presence.

The Stoic *logos* does not connote direct, clear, personal expression in the same way that our marketplace usage of "word" does. Lately, however, scholars have been busy to point out the Old Testament connections with this prologue; and as a result of those attempts, *logos* as personal expression can be seen to be very much a part of John's intention. The relationship between John's prologue and Genesis 1 has long been recognized, and we have already seen that God called the creation into being with a spoken word. *Logos* is used often in the Greek Old Testament and almost always as an active, expressive spoken word rather than an abstract principle. Above all, the prologue is best understood, not as a statement of divine and worldly principles or laws, but as the enactment of communication between God and God's people. As Raymond Brown writes, "Therefore, the emphasis is primarily on God's relation to men, rather than on God in Himself. The very title 'word' implies a revelation—not so much of a divine idea but a divine communication."[12]

If words are to have any meaning at all, they cannot be completely separated from their most elemental framework in life. So when we read this text, we should still think of Jesus as God's precious and pastoral utterance to us. And it is not so hard to imagine that utterance as being with God from the very beginning. It is a little like hearing that what someone said in his or her mature years is consistent with what he or she said and did as a youth.

> His eyes are like a flame of fire, and on his head are many diadems; and he has a name inscribed which no one knows but himself. He is clad in a robe dipped in blood, and the name by which he is called is The Word of God. (Rev. 19:12–13)

Revelation 19:11–21 describes the victory of Christ and his heavenly host over the beast and its followers. Revelation is, by its very nature, even more visual than most written books. This particular text is another vision of the great seer of Patmos. Jesus, who is seen as sitting on a white horse, is followed by the armies of heaven. His eyes are like fire, and he is clad in a robe dipped in blood. How very visual this is. Yet the name by which this great warrior is known is "the word of God," and the weapon by which he wins the victory is the sword which issues from his mouth. The materials of John's vision provide enough mystery, but a greater mystery still is the name of the rider of the white horse. The depth of that name, like the depth of personality, is known only to the rider himself.

In the New Testament, the word is sometimes understood to be God's revealed will and purpose (Luke 11:28; Rom. 9:6; Col. 1:25–27), and at other times it is understood to be the word preached by Jesus (Luke 5:1; John 5:38; John 8:55). The Christian message is described as the word of Christ (Col. 3:16), and that word is living and dynamic (Heb. 4:12) exactly because it is his living voice. The word is also a word to preach (Rom. 10:8; 2 Tim. 4:2); and Christian preaching, to complete the circle, is to preach the word which is Christ (2 Cor. 11:4; 1 Cor. 15:12; Phil. 1:15). Here we not only have the natural development of a theological idea but the identification of Jesus with the word of the creator and the creation. Now God has spoken to us in a new voice, the voice of Jesus of Nazareth, and we are called upon to take that word into our own mouths.

It is frightening to think of Jesus as *word*, just as it is frightening to think of him as someone who still comes to us in speech. There is always that longing to have something more of him than a word, something more objective, more certain. We would rather have some written-down truth that we can really get hold of. It is one type of the old dream that if we only had Jesus in flesh and blood, faith would be so much easier. But Jesus remains the Word—the word from beyond, unexpected, yet as near to us as our own breath. It is a blessing that it is so. Such a word, and it is most often a spoken word, destroys our passion for control and makes us free. It is all because the last word which God speaks to us in Jesus, the final word into that deep and dark dying time which is life, is a word of love.

THE STRANGE TALK OF PENTECOST

When the day of Pentecost had come, they were all together in one place. And suddenly a sound came from heaven like the rush of a mighty wind, and it filled all the house where they were sitting. And there appeared to them tongues as of fire, distributed and resting on each one of them. And they were all filled with the Holy Spirit and began to speak in other tongues, as the Spirit gave them utterance. (Acts 2:1–4)

Luke betrays a strong interest in the Spirit as a sign of the age of the church. At the first Pentecost, the Spirit shed abroad among believers became manifest in speech, a speech consisting of coherent languages which were also ecstatic. Pentecost marks the beginning of the new age of the risen and indwelling Christ, an age when the necessary confusion of Babel is undone by the reality and promise of the language of the Spirit.

Christians have often thought of Pentecost as the birthday of the church. From the very first day the church has been an oral community, a company constituted and motivated by the comprehensible yet free and unprecedented language of Christ's presence. The language of Pentecost provided the impulse as well as the content for the church's remarkable mission into the world.

Pentecost rates rather poorly these days among the great festivals in the actual practice of the church. Everyone seems to love Christmas. The world has clearly understood the commercial potential of a midwinter celebration; and the baby Jesus, replete with manger and assorted animals, offers a potential for romanticism which even the most austere Christian finds hard to resist. Easter is a distant second among church festivals. Yet that greatest of all early church days still promises new life in the name of the risen Christ. Even unbelievers must be curious to hear the great and joyous Easter hymns coming out from packed churches. But Pentecost just doesn't amount to much. That festival of freedom and language is frightening to settled, threatened churches that are understandably tempted to preserve their remaining strength through control and management. One pastor tried to perk up Pentecost by having the congregation release balloons as a sign of the life-giving power of the Spirit. It didn't help. Most people were just curious to see how long the balloons would stay on the ceiling.

Pentecost is the festival of speech and freedom, a festival thorn in the side of a settled church. Speech and freedom go together. Printed words can be managed, and visible elements can be hidden away until they are needed, but one never quite knows about speech. What might

someone say, and how might the words be interpreted? Settled, established churches tend to fight against the freedom of the Spirit and,
at the same time, add to the language crisis in the church. We are
surely right to be wary of the theology of some sectarian groups, but
they often have a sense of the Spirit and of language which we have
partially lost and must regain. Our theology of the Spirit is not vital,
and neither shall it be until we learn to value the precious, free character of the language of the gospel.

To say that the spoken word is held in high regard in the Bible is
to suggest that it is emphasized as one of several options. Rather, as
that which humans have most truly in common, it is simply taken for
granted as central to the life of faith. Jesus himself is identified as the
"Word." Many Christians have fallen far from the biblical conception
of the possibility of a saving, spoken word. "Fall" is the right word for
describing what has happened, in that we have willingly given ourselves over to the temptation to control and manage communication
so that no outside word can break into the reverie of our downward
gaze. Our depreciation of language is the result of sin, a preeminent
example of the decay of our culture. Fortunately, that Word which is
above all words still comes to us, and from him we may learn to speak
truly once again.

Part 3—Interpretive: Language and Interpretation

Mercury (Hermes) was the son of Jupiter and Maia. He presided over
commerce, wrestling, and other gymnastic exercises, even over thieving,
and everything, in short, which required skill and dexterity.
                              Thomas Bulfinch, *Myths of Greece and Rome*

Any discussion of the way in which the language crisis affects preaching must consider the way the crisis affects the interpretation of Scripture. Most Protestants have insisted not only that pastors should
preach, but that their preaching must be biblical. Roman Catholic
biblical scholarship is of the highest level, and many Catholics are
pushing for that scholarship to be fulfilled in a stronger emphasis on
preaching.

Luther asserted a close connection between the word of the gospel and the Bible, but he also emphasized that the written word of Scripture, if it is to become the living word of Christ for faith, most properly takes the form of public proclamation. We do have Christ in the Bible, but Christ is only known when the biblical word becomes a personal word of challenge and promise to the believing heart. That is best done in the sacraments and preaching. Conversely, if the word of preaching is not a biblical word, it is unlikely to be the word of Christ at all. The Protestant preacher is rightly pictured as preparing the sermon and preaching it from an open Bible.

Is there much biblical preaching? Leaving aside, for a moment, the knotty problem of just what it means to preach a biblical sermon, let us again be candid by asking if it seems, on the basis of present notions, that many sermons are genuinely biblical. To be sure, there is much biblical preaching, and by that preaching the church is constituted and sustained. Yet it does seem that biblical preaching is less common than it should be.

Most sermons have to do with biblical texts, but the test of a biblical sermon is whether the text becomes a lively and urgent event for the hearer. That depends upon the Holy Spirit, but all too often the sermon seems a stumbling block to, rather than a carefully crafted vehicle for, the event of the text. Preachers may speak about the text, but that is not the same as letting the text live in the sermon. Preaching about the text is closer to teaching the characteristics of the Bible. Pastors may even retell the text in the sermon, but that won't always make the text live for the modern hearer. It sometimes seems more like a journey back into Bible times, interesting but hardly crucial. Very often a preacher will use the text as a platform for personal concerns, or will just leap from the text, without delay, into the immense sea of societal analysis. If Protestants are somewhat pessimistic about the present state of preaching, then should not a call for more biblical preaching follow?

Why is it that the churches do not have enough biblical preaching? Making an ancient text live for modern hearers is a strenuous and delicate art. When that difficulty is compounded by the parishioner's inclination to want to hear only gentle, mildly affirmative news, the reason for the shortage is obvious. The point of this chapter is that the crisis in language has provided an additional, highly complicating factor for the interpretation and proclamation of biblical texts. The Bible is written, but its proclamation must be oral, a situation made to order for the sight-sound split with its attendant emphasis upon the written. Modern biblical scholarship has left the church with marvelous exegetical precision—a precision often used as the basis for the misleading rationale of finding the meaning behind the words. The words of the Bible are thought to point to truth rather than present it.

"WHAT IT MEANT AND WHAT IT MEANS"

The formula which has dominated much contemporary biblical interpretation is "what it meant and what it means." The interpreter must first determine what the biblical text meant in its original state and then decide just how those truths are to be delivered to the contemporary Christian. "What it meant and what it means" is, by its very nature, an oversimplification and certainly does not fit with some of the modern, sophisticated hermeneutical discussion. Nevertheless, on a week-in, week-out basis, that little formula has been the hermeneutical guide for many preachers. It has become an interpretive reflex, the basic intent of which can still be found lurking behind hermeneutical discussions even if the formula is never used. Let us consider what is being said here.

What it meant: The key word is *it* and in that little word, the whole formula is revealed. The text once meant something, but as an "it," a static, fixed truth. The words, which are clearly imagined to be written, fixed words rather than a lively, oral word, signify something which has become a historical deposit beyond the language itself. That deposit must be found, through exegetical examination, behind the "it" of the language of the text. The language is merely the container, and "it" takes on the character of a dead letter.

What it means: Here the key words are *it* and *means* taken together. The meaning of the text, which becomes the substance of the sermon, is cut loose from the original language. It becomes the task of the interpreter to demonstrate what the deposit of meaning is for the contemporary person. The meaning is also likely to be an "it"—a lesson to be learned rather than a living encounter. This meaning is not likely to be the gospel, because the gospel is never an "it" nor does it come from an "it." The gospel doesn't even "mean" in the sense implied here, for the gospel is always a communication event and is never divorced from language.

"What is meant and what it means" is an interpretive formula which has been produced by the sight-sound split and the crisis of language. If "what it meant" were to be taken to refer to the impact of the language event which is the text, the text would not be called an "it," and the two parts of the formula would not have to be separated. What the text meant might not be the same as what the text means. Meaning might even be just the opposite (e.g., where there are warnings about persecution), but it will be rooted in the same language event. In common practice, however, "what it meant" seeks meaning beyond the objective, but dead, written word. Certainly it is understandable that such a scheme has not tended toward lively, biblical preaching. The truth, once discovered, is simply to be given over to the hearer as sensitively but as directly as possible. If urgency and drama are not found in the language of the text, they can hardly be produced in the sermon.

The crunch of the demand of the style of interpretation that we have just described is particularly acute when it comes to preaching on the text. The system works better in the classroom than it does in the pulpit. Consider the scenario which I believe is often played out in the ministry of young pastors, especially as it relates to interpretation and preaching. The seminary student often hears over and over again about the crucial place of preaching and the importance of its being biblical. The student is carefully trained in the use of exegetical tools with which to examine texts and in the original language of the text. The idea implicit in the training is that the text will not give up its meaning easily. Meaning must be struggled over, fought for, and often found behind the pericope's language. When the student becomes ordained and takes up, among other things, the task of preaching, he or she will usually preach through pet ideas and opinions. But then, and often very soon, the question comes, "What shall I preach now?" The Bible is a welcome answer, for just then those texts hold out the promise of much-needed homiletical prompting. The young pastor sets about the business of textual preaching but soon falters over two questions: (1) Am I really skilled enough, expert enough to exegete this text? Do

I really have the specialist spectacles needed to see what is there? and
(2) What should a biblical sermon really be, anyway?

The next move is utterly predictable—the abandonment of biblical
preaching for more personal and culturally relevant sermons and a style
of ministry where the emphasis moves from proclamation to therapy
and management. This scenario may not be typical, but it is altogether
too common.

Any number of theologians are aware of the problem that we have
been describing. Some of them are moving interpretation away from
the pitfalls attendant upon the simple formula "what it meant and what
it means." It is somewhat unusual, however, to think through the issue
primarily in terms of the crisis of language. In fact, it may well be that
the reason why the basic principles of "what it meant and what it
means" are so tenacious is their logical connection with the sound-sight
split.

ELEMENTS IN AN INTERPRETIVE PROCESS
LUKE 1:26–38—THE ANNUNCIATION

How enjoyable and easy it is to speak of the way things should not
be! The task of saying what should be is nearly always more difficult.
The time has come, however, to ask just how one reads a text as a
living, oral word, and to notice what some implications of such a reading
are. A sense for a text as a living, oral word depends on an intuition
about language which is not readily available in today's marketplace,
an intuition which we simply cannot have in the same way that less
typographic peoples can. At the same time, we are people who speak,
and that means that the capacity for an oral reading is as near as our
daily communication.

To begin, the interpreter must try to think of the text as a living,
urgent dialogue rather than a fixed, objective record. Reading a text
with great care and a sense for the ebb and flow of life there, almost
as one would read a good novel, is the best start. There are many
amazing details at the beginning of the annunciation; but everything
moves toward the angelic greeting, a greeting which is not so wondrous
because it is angelic, but because of its content and the lowly status
of the one to whom it is given.

Mary is troubled by Gabriel's words. Perhaps she senses that these words, which she does not yet fully understand, will dramatically change her life. The increasingly personal character of the conversation between this obscure woman and Gabriel moves toward her reassurance, "Do not be afraid." Mary need not be afraid for, while one may be afraid of a task or even a designation, one can scarcely be afraid of an exaltation so great as to become the mother of a son who will be the savior. Even in v. 31, however, where Jesus' name is mentioned, it is still Mary's fear which is the preoccupation. When the credentials of the son to be born to her are presented in vv. 32–33, it only serves to enhance her lowly status as over against her new calling.

Mary guarantees the unlikely character of the annunciation by saying that she has no husband. Immediately her incredulity is countered by the angel's promise that this will be God's own work, a gift of the Spirit. Then, as though Mary's wavering faith needed some sign for encouragement, Gabriel tells her that Elizabeth, her kinswoman, has conceived a son in her old age. With that, the lowly Mary forgets her unworthiness and capitulates in faith, saying, "Let it be to me according to your word."

Attention must be given to the details of the language, both because language is made up of particular parts and for the same reason that one does well to notice a lifted eyebrow in a conversation. In v. 26, the lowly and humble character of Mary is augmented by the mention of Nazareth, a little village of no account. Gabriel's announcement is to come to a virgin, for the fulfillment of the promise is to be directly and powerfully God's own work. Yet Mary was betrothed to a man who was of the house of David. While God is about to do a new thing through Mary, God is still the God of Israel. The word "hail" in v. 28 not only is a royal greeting but also carries the additional meaning of "rejoice" or "be glad." Just as the name "Mary" is used in v. 30 to ensure the personal character of Gabriel's word of comfort, so also Luke attaches great significance to the name Jesus, which means "God saves." The compact and powerful catalog of messianic credentials given in vv. 32–33 reflects various Old Testament passages (2 Sam. 7:13–16; Ps. 89:26–29; Psalm 2; Micah 4:7). The point is that the child to be born to Mary will be well qualified to be Israel's messiah. When Mary questions the angel's promise because she has not known a man intimately

(v. 34), Gabriel responds with words that form a powerful parallelism: "The Holy Spirit will come upon you, and the power of the Most High will overshadow you." Because it is the Holy Spirit that will bring about this birth in Mary, the child will be called "holy," one set apart in the service of God, one who is literally the "son of God."

Careful readers will keep the context of a passage in mind precisely because it is the cradle for the language event under consideration. A major contextual emphasis from Luke's Gospel particularly important for the interpretation of the annunciation is in the way that the third evangelist radically shifts the criteria for membership in the kingdom. "The high and the mighty, including especially those who might be classified as the religious establishment, have no assured automatic claim to the kingdom. God reaches out to the lowly, the outcasts, women, 'tax collectors and sinners.' "[13] These form a large percentage out of which God fashions the social register.

The more immediate context in chapter one includes news of another birth, that of John, which serves to dramatize the birth of Jesus. There is just enough similarity between the two announcement stories to heighten the contrast on behalf of Mary. Zechariah and Elizabeth were old and she was barren, but Mary was young, obscure, and had never known a man. An angel appeared to both Zechariah and Mary, and both were afraid, but John's job was to prepare the people for the Lord, whereas Jesus was to be "the son of the Most High." Both women became pregnant, but only one child is the direct issue of the spirit of God, and it is Elizabeth who lauds Mary as blessed among women— an old woman of some distinction praising a youthful, unknown maid.

Above all, the reader should keep the usual, oral characteristics of language in mind. What is the text saying? What is surprising, convicting, promising about the episode of the text? How might the same conversation have gone today? Where does the narrative take a turn that you wouldn't expect? In the case of the annunciation, the surprising turn is defined by the contrast between the angelic messenger with his exalted announcement and the lowly Mary. God is about to draw very near to us, as near as this ordinary maid, who at the end of the annunciation says, "I am the handmaid of the Lord; let it be to me according to your word." Thus Mary becomes what many have called a model of faith. Yes, and much more than a model, for we best remember Mary as the mother of Jesus, that One whose word comes to us now to awaken and sustain faith. How strange that God should come into the lowly place which is our lives.

Taken so, the interpreter may begin to have some sense for what the text means without having to go through that former first step of what it meant. How can we know what a language event really meant, any more than we can be sure of what a childhood conversation meant? But if a record of a childhood conversation is made known to us, one can have a sense of what that conversation means now. Even to imagine what it meant then is to reflect the conversation's present meaning into the past.

EXEGESIS AND INTERPRETATION

Our attempts to unlock the meaning of the fixed, written words of the Bible have often eventuated in control of the text rather than lively, public proclamation. Control is important, although only to let the text speak. The historical character of God's revelation in Christ makes it impossible for the Bible to mean something unique, subjective, and private for each interpreter. If we learn to do better at taking Scripture seriously as a living language event, what is to guard against complete subjectivism? A detailed grammatical study of the text for one thing, and the self-conscious inclusion of systematic theology within a confessing community for another.

Historical-critical exegesis has served the enterprise of biblical study well. Never before has such scholarly care been taken over the language and context of Scripture. However, historical-critical exegesis has produced problems as well as blessings. Texts are sometimes dismembered with such exactitude that they can never be put back together again. Any possibility of a healthy, living, breathing language encounter is lost. The problem seems not so much with the historical-critical method as with its traditional, main presupposition—that exegesis must find the actual history behind the written word. Because the written word most often has priority over the spoken in our society, there is a suspicion that all language signifies something "back there." That presupposition must be abandoned.

However, a new sense of Scripture as a living word must not imply less concern for the particulars of the text. If anything, the text and context must now be taken more seriously than ever—more seriously precisely because the words are considered to be communication events and not arrows pointing beyond. Ernst Fuchs, in commenting on a new approach to biblical language, writes, "Of course I do not deny that these are historical facts, nor do I deny that historical criticism is a good way to establish facts. One cannot treasure too highly the empirical, the factually provable. Anyone who has flown even once in an airplane sees this point. Here in the airplane only facts count. Hence a crash is an awful thing which always makes everyone sad. This is also true in the area of the New Testament. I do not think we should rank the facts lower. Rather I think we should note facts even more carefully than we are accustomed to do in the practice of exegesis and preaching."[14]

What is the nature of biblical sermons? We have already said that sermons are not for the purpose of handing scriptural truths over to the hearer. What then? Confessional theology teaches that it is to "do" the text for the hearer. (That is the language of my friend and colleague Gerhard Forde, and it seems a good way to state the matter.) The object of the sermon is to establish an occasion whereby the contemporary challenge, offense, and promise of the text is heard by a congregation. The claim of the text now becomes a living, present claim in the mouth of the preacher. The sermon does not seem to be about the pericope, and its character is not primarily didactic. Nor does one always realize that the sermon is being made scriptural in its preaching. It is often only in retrospect that one can say that the work which the text does on a hearer has not been done "*pro me.*" Even though it is risky and inadvisable, it is nonetheless possible to imagine a very textual sermon where the text is never once mentioned.

The similarity between preaching and hearing poetry read or going to a play is obvious. Language is living, present, urgent in all three. The words of a poem or play, however, always remain the same, and in a sermon everything in the text may need to be translated for the sake of the "*de profundis*" of the gospel. It is perhaps more appropriate to compare a sermon with a musical composition where the theme has been taken from another work. The two compositions are by no means identical, but that former theme is made to sound with particular and vital beauty in the new. The sermon is not to be about the pericope but to do the text for today's world.

HERMENEUTICS AND LANGUAGE

The science of interpretation has proven to be less scientific than we once thought. The problem is by no means the capacity for detail which attends the historical-critical method, for one can never pay too much attention to the detail of language. The problem is the presupposition that written texts have left their life in the historical deposit that lies behind them. Even written texts refuse the precision of surgical investigation, for they maintain something of the character of the living discourse of a community. We have learned that art and imagination are as necessary to interpretation as is science. The text is not an object to be investigated but a living voice from the past which refuses to remain silent in the present.

Among theologians and linguists, the debate over interpretation is shifting away from the realm of historical-critical investigation toward a concern for how language works. The present concern is not so much whether an ancient text can mean something today as it is concern over just how an ancient word works on a contemporary hearer. Scholars wonder just how language, even the language of Jesus, does its stuff: just how does it call new reality into being. The scientific investigation of the text is being replaced by the scientific analysis of how language works. The new hermeneutics, when confined to a discussion of how language works, hardly offers the church new life for interpretation. Instead, attention to context and detail can be lost to random subjectivity.

Perhaps some clues for a good and lively hermeneutic can be gained by recalling elements from the life of Hermes, that Greek god after whom the interpretive enterprise is named. A complete interpreter certainly can't be modeled upon the distant figure of the crafty Hermes, but some of the characteristics of that good-humored messenger can set us moving in new hermeneutical directions, directions away from the static confines of fixed words toward listening for a lively voice.

Hermes was the god of boundaries, not as one who was confined by conventional geographical bounds but as one who could move easily from one region to another. Two territories might be separated for their respective residents, even forbidden, but Hermes could pass from one to the other and back again as easily as the wind. Yet, as the one who transcended boundaries, Hermes also protected and guarded them. In all of this Hermes was not droll or burdensome but of good spirit, the most pleasant of the gods. The interpreter has boundaries to cross, boundaries both of dialect and time, but cross them we can. The task need not be dull or burdensome; for listening for another voice is most often engaging, and the Christian listens for a voice that has saving power.

Hermes was nimble, crafty, deft, ingenious, and sometimes deceitful. Yet Hermes' dexterity was not used to harm those with whom he had to do, but only to deliver more effectively a message from another god or guide the traveler along a difficult path. Hermes' approach could rarely be predicted. Most often he would appear suddenly, surprisingly; and when in his company, one was apt to be further surprised by such a lucky event as finding valuables along the path. Creativity is certainly necessary for the interpreter who constructs a sermon, but some deftness is also required in reading texts, if only the eager expectation of hearing a voice from beyond and not quite knowing what that voice will say. When the gospel comes, it is always a surprise, ever new.

Hermes was also the messenger, the herald, and god of eloquence who once won a verbal battle with Stentor and gave Pandora her voice.[15] It is no accident that when Paul came to Lystra, where he and Barnabas were mistaken for gods, Paul, as the chief speaker, was called Hermes (Acts 14:12). In the oral culture of classical Greece, the interpreter was also one who spoke, for the knowledge gained from interpretation was not meant for private keeping but was to be relayed to the community. Paul did not object to being called Hermes on the grounds of not being a herald, but because he had good news of another—one not called Hermes but Jesus. Can the Christian interpreter of Scripture find some knowledge there which takes its place in the history of the world? Of course! But the heart of the communication of the Scriptures is a very personal word, a saving word which is near you and takes on the power of the Spirit in the breath of the telling. Exegesis without interpretation is impossible, and interpretation without proclamation denies the living voice of Christ.

Above all, Hermes was too nimble and agile to be caught.[16] The word of the message which this god brought was a living word which maintained its power into the future in spite of being expended on every occasion of its hearing. Once heard, it could be heard again and again as a new, fresh voice. Hermes had wings on his feet because his words could fly. Pastors often assume that ancient texts, preached on again and again, have a new and living voice because the situation of the hearer has changed. Is it simply the passage of time and the emergence of new generations that keeps a text, once mined of its historical truth, from becoming a dead letter? In reality, biblical texts remain a living language voice in search of a hearer, a voice which seeks to break in upon us from beyond, a word which cannot be caught in any hearing. Just as the risen Christ is the present Christ, closer to us than we are to ourselves, so also his word lives as the event of the gospel, not bound by history but shaping the present and future in the form of God. Listening for that word is by no means dull and lackluster, but a considerable joy.

4
The Word in the Church's Life

Part 1—The Problem of Language and Christian Worship

O come, let us worship and bow down,
   let us kneel before the LORD, our Maker!
For he is our God,
   and we are the people of his pasture,
   and the sheep of his hand.
                                        (Ps. 95:6-7)

Worship is at the heart of Christian living. Although a devaluation of speech certainly affects the daily vocation of Christians, the problem which that dilemma affords for Christians is bound to be particularly noticeable in worship. Worship has been defined as God speaking to us in Word and Sacrament and our speaking to God in prayer and praise. Such a definition presumes that the church is an oral community. It follows that if the spoken word is devalued, Christian worship will be directly threatened. One has only to reflect on random aspects of Christian worship to see how it is so.

PRAYER

This subject has not had much attention in formal, theological discussion (but see A *Primer on Prayer*, ed. Paul Sponheim, Fortress Press, 1988). Perhaps it is most often sufficient to remember the command and example of Jesus. But prayer, like all matters of faithful worship, is not an easy thing to do well. Prayer is threatened by the various doubts attendant upon unbelief and by the crisis of language in the church. Thinking of prayer from the perspective of oral speech can help clear away some of the obstacles in the path of our "talks with God."

"Talking with God" was one definition that many of us learned for prayer, and however simple, it is a good one. The idea is a conversation as lively, as personal, as urgent, as fitting for the occasion as that between a parent and a child at the end of a busy day—only this conversation is with God. What a beautiful and compelling prospect! But even a talk with God depends upon language, and we have no other words than those we use in our daily rounds. Thus, the general societal problems over language can be seen to infringe upon our prayer life in at least three ways:

1. If talk does seem to be cheap, it is not surprising that we wonder if talk with God won't be the same. God is not to blame. The nature of the communion itself, which we assume to be a concession to "our side," appears to be unworthy. Or, to move the issue in another direction just slightly, if our usual talk is necessarily cheap, what kind of language can we find to speak with God? If we seek a language more churchly, more exalted, we shall find that we have only our ordinary tongue. Only as God gives us a renewed love for language and breathes new vitality into all our conversation will we find it easier to pray.

2. Christians believe that God knows the heart or, as we are more apt to put it, that God "sees" into the heart. If language is the conveyance of thoughts and sentiments that are "written on the heart," then prayer is merely to rehearse before God what God already knows. If one assumes that language is to give information when God has all the information already, there is little motivation for the language of prayer. Our only consolation is that in prayer we will learn to know ourselves better. Prayer becomes an exercise in introspection, a monologue without anyone to hear or respond. The wildly general definition of prayer as an "attitude of all life," which is so common these days, gains some of its impetus from our fear that a conversation, especially when it is with a God who already knows us, wouldn't amount to anything. Such a general definition is a long way from the more proper notion of "talking with God."

The words of our prayers are not containers to transmit thoughts and sentiments which God already knows. In our words we come into being. Our life unfolds and is realized in language. In the language of prayer, the faithful Christian is called forth and nourished within the environment of self-conscious conversation with the Creator. Prayer is a full and eager communion with that one who daily provides for and sustains us. That conversation is new life for us, not merely a rehearsal of what is static and complete. Prayer is new life before God too, for God is by no means done with creative work within us. In a genuine visit with God, which may have many of the characteristics of a visit with a friend, God breathes new life into us through our words. Prayer is not to "tell" God or "come before God," but to live most fully and intimately with God. Just as life unfolds in conversation with our family and friends, so also it is most properly and beautifully created and sustained by visits with that one who has been and continues to be the source of our being.

3. The problem of language also has considerable bearing on what we think God's answer to prayer might be. Genuine conversation cannot be one-sided; there must be a hearing and a response. That is also true of our talks with God. How will God answer our prayers? If our words are merely vessels containing inner, objective sentiments and thoughts, God can only answer by giving us greater self-knowledge or "objective" blessings. A search for "objective" answers is particularly confusing. God sends blessings to all people, and it is often difficult to know how specific events relate to particular prayers. If one falls into the trap of casting about for a dramatic or spectacular answer to prayer, it will most often seem that God has not heard or responded.

If prayer is "talking to God," then we might expect that God's most proper form of answer would be to talk back to us. When one visits with another, it is reasonable to expect that there will be some word of response. God, for our sakes, responds to the words of our prayers with the word of the proclamation of the gospel, the word of the sacraments, and the words of other believers. To be sure, God may bring about what we think of as an objective event in answer to our prayer, and we may be given faith to see it as such. But most properly, God answers our words with God's own word of the gospel, a word which makes the conversation complete. Just as our lives are actualized by language, so also the word of the gospel is truly life giving and sets us free. There is no greater answer to prayer than to hear that word and know that it is "for me," and by that word all other more "objective" answers to prayer are interpreted and understood.

SILENCE AND WORSHIP

Protestants are uncomfortable with silence during worship. When a prescribed period of liturgical silence occurs, Protestants are apt to look around as though wondering what is actually supposed to be happening. Is it simply a lack of poise? Hardly, for the Protestant is a member of an oral community where silence seems unnatural and doesn't have an obvious theological justification. If language is at the center of worship, how can liturgical silence be justified?

Apart from the obvious need for private and personal prayer, silence has been justified from several points of view. Silence is thought to be a listening for the inner voice, the voice of the private self. Self-examination is important, and it may even have some part in the silence of worship, but most often the self is best revealed by a word from beyond. Although people are the crown of the creation, as fallen creatures we have no saving word within ourselves. Redemptive words must come from another. The inner voice, if it is the voice of our feelings, isn't to be trusted. That voice can lie like everything. If silence is listening for the true, inner voice of the private self, it has little justification in Christian worship.

Silence is sometimes thought to be representative of the hiddenness of God. Just as God, as spirit, is not available to our senses, so also God is concealed in silence. This cannot be a theological basis for liturgical silence because we know God precisely as the one who has spoken and does speak to us in the word of the Son. It is in that common but extraordinary word that God is hidden. God is not hidden in a distant silence but in the word of Jesus which is very near. The concealment of Christ doesn't need to be proven or actualized liturgically. That concealment will take care of itself.

Sometimes liturgical silence is justified as a moment of reverence or respect for God. Silence of respect takes two forms in the family of humankind. On the one hand, it is a custom to observe a moment of silence for someone who is dead. It is a moment of respect, but respect for one who is now dead and can no longer speak. Speaking to someone who cannot respond would be utterly disrespectful. Silence of respect is not an attempt at communion so much as a recognition of a life that has ended, a last and temporary joining in the condition of one who is now perfectly silent. Silence as the sound of death has little place as the actualization of respect for a living God. On the other hand, there are those communication theorists who contend that the most intimate communion between people persists in silence. Instead of a discussion of the inner world of feeling, needs, and aspirations, for example, there is simply a mystical, mutual intuition between two people. Perhaps people who know each other well can achieve this mystical, silent identity, but certainly we cannot claim such a union with God. God is God, after all, and sufficiently unlike us so that conventional empathy seems insufficient reason for liturgical silence.

To find a justification for liturgical silence in an oral community, it is best to consider how silence actually works among people. Sometimes sustained silence among loved ones is the most cruel state of all, a mark of the complete disintegration of communication. Everyone knows that the "cold silent treatment" is terribly frustrating and deadly. On other occasions, however, silence serves to augment the constructive speech of community. People cannot be talking all the time. They must have rest even from that most natural form of community. Silence of this sort is the antiphon of speech, representative of the silence out of which a word from the other must come. Silence has no word, no saving power of its own, but silence can be one way of respecting the vital power of those words which must come to us if we are to live.

Silence within a church which is defined as an oral community has great value as an antiphon for speech. Liturgical placement should therefore come at those points in the service where silence serves to amplify the specific declaration of the gospel.

THE SACRAMENTS

The sacraments are being emphasized with renewed vigor these days. Instructional materials abound with references to Baptism, and there is a proper, although easily misinterpreted, emphasis on the life that the baptized person should lead within the community of the church. Baptism is above all God's gracious deed of promise. The Lord's Supper is celebrated in our churches much more than it has been in the recent past, with some churches offering that sacrament each week. The sacraments, as means of grace, should not need a special emphasis within the community which they call into being. Nevertheless, they are a particularly appropriate antidote for the lonely individualism of our time. Any age that is as preoccupied as ours with individual rights and freedom is bound to be a lonely time. The sacraments are welcome acts of belonging.

An emphasis on the sacraments combined with a general, cultural depreciation of language can, however, push Christian understanding and practice in unfortunate directions.

There are two miniature descriptions of the sacraments which can be placed under productive theological analysis relative to the crisis of language. The first is the description of the sacrament as "visible word," and the second is that of the word acting with the water, bread, and wine.

The sacrament as visible word: this is a confusing phrase. Certainly it does not refer to the written word, which is visible; nor does it refer to the spoken word which can be seen, since it surely cannot. Neither should visible word be thought of as a complete assimilation of word and, for example, water. After all, you can wash with one and order groceries with the other, but not vice versa. Yet, just as the spoken word is embodied and visible in the one who speaks, so also the sacramental word is embodied in the speaker and in the ordinary elements of water, bread, and wine. In this sense one can speak of a visible word. Robert Jenson writes, "Therefore the Lutherans prevented rivalry between word and sacraments by a move quite different from that of Zwingli and the spiritualists: the Lutherans interpreted the sacraments as *themselves* words, as themselves communication-events. Augustine has defined a sacrament as a visible word, and this definition had become standard in the medieval tradition; the Lutherans adopted it to their purpose. A sacramental act, *as a whole event,* just *is* a word, a mutual address of those involved, an event that says something— which something is, of course, to be the gospel."[1]

As long as we are clear about what our purpose is in the use of Augustine's definition, it is fine. But in a time of a crisis in language, it is common to understand "visible word" to imply that the communicating word of the gospel has been replaced by the visible fact of

water, bread, or wine. These elements, after all, are sure and certain
in a way that the spoken word is not. A tacit denial of the place of the
spoken word in deference to more physical and objective elements is
never far from idolatry. Idolatry, in these times, longs for a visual
element because the unseen word of speech hardly tempts our devotion. Any veteran pastor knows how easy it is to be discouraged with
words, and how tempting it is to believe that in the visible elements
there is a certainty of grace beyond the word of promise.

In his Small Catechism, Luther says this about Baptism: "It is not
water that does these things, but God's Word with the water." That
simple statement is filled with theological genius and, in a time of a
crisis of language, is an absolutely necessary correlative of the definition
of sacrament as "visible word." Here the word and the elements are
not separated but joined under the command of Christ. Just as the
spoken word is actualized by and becomes visible in its speaker, so
also the word of the sacrament is actualized by and becomes visible in
the speaker and the water, bread, or wine. So long as the word remains
the word of promise, the freedom of grace is preserved and idolatry
is avoided. Neither can it be understood that the elements add to or
assist the word. That would have the irony of making the sacraments
superior to preaching but the elements merely additions to the word.
The elements become a part of the embodiment of the word, insep-
arable and yet distinct. The sacrament is thus truly described as an
event of the word of the gospel.

Just as the word of promise and the elements are firmly joined in
Luther's theology of the sacraments, so also must that union be born
out in liturgical practice. The more difficult problem is knowing just
what words should be said, and how many. Some of the words can be
about the elements in the sacraments, rehearsing the place that bread,
wine, and water have in the Scriptures and in our common life. In
current Lutheran practice there is a good deal of such language about
the water of Baptism. But language should not be used in a way which
detracts from the oral word of promise. It is the word of the promise
of God, together with the elements, that gives the sacraments unity
and power to faith. That word can be very short: "This is my body,"
"This is my blood," "I baptize you in the name of the Father, the Son,
and the Holy Spirit." Nevertheless, a longer formula, which is not too

preoccupied with bread, wine, or water, and where the word of promise is central, can serve the pastor and congregation by easing the temptation to idolize the physical elements.

Part 2—Words, the Word, and Preaching

Where is the wise man? Where is the scribe? Where is the debater of this age? Has not God made foolish the wisdom of the world? For since, in the wisdom of God, the world did not know God through wisdom, it pleased God through the folly of what we preach to save those who believe. For Jews demand signs and Greeks seek wisdom, but we preach Christ crucified, a stumbling block to Jews and folly to Gentiles, but to those who are called, both Jews and Greeks, Christ the power of God and the wisdom of God. For the foolishness of God is wiser than men, and the weakness of God is stronger than men. (1 Cor. 1:20–25)

We have come to the point where our implicit concern for preaching must be made explicit. The church is an oral community in a broad sense, but there is no greater mark of that orality than the emphasis which the church gives to the public proclamation of the gospel. It is left to us now to inquire about the way that the language crisis impinges on preaching and, more positively, to say something about what our knowledge of language teaches us concerning the nature of the interpretation of texts and the shape of a sermon. Preaching, as an act of the whole person, cannot be easily taught. If any parish preacher, or someone who regularly listens to sermons, should find encouragement or insight here, it will make the effort worthwhile.

PREACHING:
GENUINE DIALOGUE?

Genuine communication is, by definition, rooted in dialogue. At least two parties must be involved, each with something at stake in the communion, each with something to contribute. It is not possible to think of genuine oral communion as involving one active and one totally passive participant. Preaching often seems to be hopelessly one-sided. It is, at best, considered an authoritarian word which does not allow for response, or at worst, an irrelevant word which does not deserve any. The question is clear: can preaching be considered real communication? The amount of current interest in "talk-back" sessions following the sermon gives evidence that pastors feel this predicament keenly.

A conviction that preaching is one-sided per se is grounded in a misunderstanding of the nature of oral communication. It is commonly assumed that to have dialogue, both parties must speak, whereas the basic act of communication is in speaking and hearing. Every pastor has preached sermons that are one-sided in the sense of being of no concern to the hearer. But when the preached word is truly heard, there is full communication. The two poles of oral discourse are speaking and hearing, not speaking and speaking. Eventually, of course, the hearer will have a chance to speak, but that is not what makes the communion complete. Martin Buber has written, "But what then lends this priority to the spoken word? Is not what we take from the present continuance of language in order to think it, or what we take from the possession of language in order to read it, often incalculably superior to the spoken word? The importance of the spoken word, I think, is grounded in the fact that it does not want to remain with the speaker. It reaches out toward a hearer, it lays hold of him, it even makes the hearer into a speaker, if perhaps only a soundless one."[2] Preaching, when there is genuine hearing, is full communication. Is it possible that our emphasis upon speaking to speaking is another way to make communication objective, in the same way that print is given priority over speech?

SERMON AND LANGUAGE STRUCTURE

Preachers have been wary of paying much attention to sermon structure. Just as it has been assumed that the words of a text are the husk to hold the kernel of the text's meaning, so also it has seemed that the structure of the sermon is primarily the container for the preacher's message. If one finds the meaning behind the text, it has been assumed that the meaning can be successfully delivered in almost any shape or form. Many preachers have been terribly afraid of technique in preaching. Some of that fear, of course, is warranted. Inappropriate concern for structure and language can result in sermons that are cute, self-centered, and manipulative in a wrong way. In the period of orthodoxy, preachers did seem to be overly concerned with structure, and many of them turned out sermons governed by a mechanical understanding of law and gospel.

Nowadays, however, it is difficult for preachers to ignore the flood of evidence that meaning cannot be separated from the words and structure of the sermon. The words of the sermon and the way that those words are put together constitute its message. The way that something is said is the actual saying of it.

It must now be asked if there are particular forms which are especially suited to oral discourse and "doing" the text in a sermon. Are there certain linguistic patterns which can be of consistent help to the preacher? Is there some form of rhetoric, itself born out of oral discourse, which is useful in constituting sermons which serve the gospel? Certainly many linguistic forms can be helpful to the preacher, but dialectic, properly defined and with a Lutheran twist, can be particularly helpful in giving true, oral life to a sermon.

A DEFINITION OF DIALECTIC

Dialectic, although it has become a highly specialized word, does have a marketplace definition. It is thought to refer to a "logical examination of ideas to test their validity." That definition is a product of the sight-sound split and is not centrally useful for preaching. The sense which such a definition of dialectic gives is of ideas all lined up in a row to be examined in the light of clear reason. Good preaching needs clear thinking, but logic is not the primary form of oral discourse.

We must move behind the modern definition to the practice of dialectic in the Middle Ages. Dialectic, with grammar and rhetoric, was one part of the trivium, or main curriculum, of study, rooted in orality and taught in an oral way. Dialectic was an examination of ideas, and was as such given to logical analysis, but an examination which was argued out in public discussion. Logic was not the detached observation of so many ideas lined up in a row, but the logic of a sensible reality achieved through oral exchange. The natural polemical character of oral communication was amplified in the "yes" and "no" of oral debate. The freedom of normal dialogue was amplified by the adjustments made in moving toward a resolution, a freedom which is not so evident in today's highly stylized, academic debates. Above all, the coming-to-birth and dying which is typical of life and thus of genuine conversation was heightened by the polarity of the discussion.

Dialectic had most of the characteristics of life. It is quite understandable that Hegel used dialectic to describe the reciprocating engine which powers history. In order to invest dialectic with a useful definition, we would do well to think of a case that is being argued out in court. There is search, challenge, question, response, movement, and resolution—in short, all the characteristics of life and of urgent communication.

How might dialectic, in terms of the spare definition just given, affect the shape of the sermon? First of all, even when dealing with the details of the text, the interpreter will remember that the text was and is intended to be a communication event. The preacher will listen for the challenge of the text, the "yes" and the "no," and a resolution. (If the resolution of the text is not explicit, it is implicit. Christians believe that all of the Bible is about Jesus.) From the very beginning, the interpreter will also imagine the dialectical elements which the text might raise in the lives of modern hearers. What is the struggle in the text? What is surprising? How does the text say no to the hearer? How does it say yes? How is the text offensive to the way things work in the world? The whole interpretive process is not so much like a search for hidden treasure as it is a struggle with one who seems like an adversary but who turns out to be quite the opposite.

Dialectic, however, is best thought of as one element in the form of a sermon, rather than the structure itself. The actual form might be a three-point sermon, an exposition which marches through the text, a sermon with large amounts of story, or a sermon where the answering back and forth of dialectic is explicit. Whatever the form, dialectic should be characteristic of it rather than dictatorial. Where dialectic is explicit, particular care must be taken so that the argument doesn't become wooden, obvious, and predictable.

In any structure, dialectic guarantees that the terrain of the sermon will not be flat. There must be some hills, some curves in the road, and even some surprises behind the trees. The sermon becomes contrapuntal, living between the yes and the no of the text, stretched out on the tension between affirmation and negation. Some kind of rhetorical coming-to-birth and dying is played out right in the proclamation. The sermon has the character of an argument, but not an argument such as in teaching, where the lecturer moves toward a conclusion by the linear development of supporting evidence. Rather, this is an argument where every objection, every scandal, every offense is taken absolutely seriously; when the resolution comes, it does so as the only alternative left.

DIALECTIC WITH A LUTHERAN TWIST

Thus far we have spoken of dialectic in very general terms. The contention has been made that dialectic might affect the shape of the sermon to advantage, but we still haven't raised the issue of how dialectic can serve the gospel. After all, it's easy to imagine how dialectic could make the sermon vague and cryptic. The next step is to give dialectic a Lutheran twist and in four ways.

1. Homiletical use of dialectic is informed by an understanding of law and gospel. When someone hears the word of Christ, that word is heard either as law or good news. For example, when the listener hears the words "Blessed are the meek," they cannot be heard as anything other than good or bad news. The faithless hearer, at worst, considers the way in which the world reviles meekness or, at best, considers how meekness might well be a desirable characteristic of personality. The faithful hearer, who knows what it means to be meek in repentance before a holy God, hears the beatitude as gospel and is truly blessed. The freedom of the gospel, which is the freedom of its hearing, cannot be denied by the preacher.

It seems reasonable that the hearing both of the law and of the gospel must be explicitly provided for in the sermon—one side of the dialectic clearly stating the law, and the other, the gospel. Such an explicit rendering is, however, only advisable when a message of sheer commandment is being combined with its correlative message of promise (i.e., "Thou shalt not steal" with "Jesus loves thieves"). When the point of the sermon is directly and solely a gospel word, the elements of the dialectic should be formed to allow the promise to ring as clearly as possible, which ringing can then be heard as either good or bad news.

In this latter case law is not made explicit, and the dialectic is most often found in the tension between the promise and its offense.

2. The dialectical elements in the sermon should not be arranged according to the logic of conventional argument but as mortal enemies. In most forms of persuasive discourse, the evidence is lined up or massed in such a way so as to convince. The parts of the argument are complementary and lead from one to the other. In a good sermon, however, the parts of the dialectic stand in stark contrast, deadly enemies to the very end. They simply cannot be mixed or blended. Thus, the gospel is not won by the logic of the sermon but appears as something unique and surprising. It's hard for the preacher to fight linear, logical argumentation—to fight being a good speech-maker. One cannot find many hints in written documents to help with understanding dialectical enmity, but clues can be found in oral discourse.

3. The dialectical elements of the sermon should not be confused. Whereas we referred to the placement of major units of language in the previous point, here we are talking about language itself. The language of the law cannot be diluted to suggest that anything more is needed. If the two are confused, the gospel is lost first, then the law. Confusion most often occurs when the law is thought to take the hearer partway to blessedness, with the gospel finishing the job. A good example would be preaching meekness as a goal of Christian behavior, to be rewarded by the blessing of the gospel.

4. The dialectical elements of law and gospel, in addition to being provided, separated, and not confused, must also be arranged so as to keep people from returning to the law and death. Luther knew that people, left to their own devices, turn to the law. We tend to prefer that which is familiar and conventional, even if it means the end. For example, we may be comforted to know that the world does not reward meekness, or that some who seem to be meek are really passive-aggressive, or that meekness is a condition of personality which can only be gained by persistent resolve. It is the homiletical version of the death wish.

Rightly dividing law and gospel in this instance means defining and arranging material in such a way so as to head off the hearer whenever there is a turn toward the law. It is to strip away every worldly condition, every "if then" which the hearer wants to hang on the gospel in order to dilute its promise and claim. Robert Jenson writes, "Rightly dividing the law and the gospel is the knack of so making promises in Jesus' name as endlessly to transcend this turn back to the law. 'God loves you for Jesus' sake.' 'Yes, if I could only believe that. But I can't.' To which the gospel sayer who knows his job responds, 'Just by your unbelief you prove yourself the very man whom God loves, for he chooses above all, the ungodly!' "[3]

By these four adjustments dialectic is given a law-gospel character. These definitions and distinctions are difficult enough to understand, and once understood, it seems impossible that they could ever be put into homiletical practice. When compared to a linear, visually oriented sense for preaching, dialectic seems terribly difficult. Yet the notion of dialectic is as close as our everyday speech. It is not surprising that when this particular emphasis has been described, there are many pastors who will rightly realize that they have been preaching this very way all along.

A WAY TO DIALECTIC

The gospel occurs as a linguistic event having the character of proclamation. It is like a physician's announcement of good news to parents who have been anxiously waiting outside the sickroom of their child. Although the gospel is not a two-sided word, dialectic is helpful in capturing the urgent, oral character of announcement and in representing, through homiletical form, the way in which the gospel will be heard.

Thus far, our discussion of dialectic has been formal. Now we must talk about how homiletical content can be gathered from text and congregation to make up the dialectical language of a sermon. Be assured that to examine a particular text in this way doesn't imply that the same message will always be found. Dialectic isn't the message but a way of speaking the message. Content can be obtained in two ways: in the juxtaposition of commandment and gospel, and in the juxtaposition of the offense of the gospel and the gospel. In each case the text is thought of as an oral confrontation with the hearers. Rather than being considered as separate halves, text and hearers are together from the very beginning.

COMMANDMENT AND THE GOSPEL

The combination of commandment and word of promise is a necessary, if not most common, way of shaping homiletical dialectic. (Command, used here, not only refers to the Ten Commandments, but to all texts that function as a "Thou shalt not!") When command is combined with promise in any way other than through dialectic, the two will complement and blend into one another. That is simply not the way either command or promise functions as a communication event. The two are enemies and must be kept separate.

Students of preaching often ask if the commandment should sometimes be preached alone, as a brisk, negative word. Perhaps so, but only if the situation demands it or, in extreme cases, if the preacher's patience with the congregation has completely run out. If the command of God is preached apart from the promise often, the preacher is likely to cultivate spiritual problems among the hearers.

Problems occur in two ways. On the one hand, the message can become too dark and devastating for the conscientious listener, with no way out of the trap. On the other hand, the command might begin to sound like something which gives life and sets the believer free. The law begins to sound like a friend. Because life must have limits and because the commandments can serve something better, the law is a friend. But it is a friendship that will not last. Too much preaching of the command apart from the promise is like harsh, parental advice without an environment of care and affection.

What if the text, which may be full of austere command, does not have any promise? What of the promise side of the dialectic then? Remember that all biblical texts lead to Jesus. The text must be taken with complete seriousness, and just so is Christ found to be implicit if not explicit in it. Jesus is not at the beginning of the law texts, or in the middle, but at the end, when the text has fully run its course.

Old Testament pericopes, which by no means contain only law, seem to pose a particular problem. When the command of God does appear in Old Testament texts, preaching a text in dialectic with the good news of Jesus appears to impose Jesus on the material. That can, unfortunately, be done, but it is not a necessary result of our method. If the Old Testament is thought of as a fixed, written record bound to its pre-Christian past, it obviously is not right to add anything to it. But if the text is considered a living language event, the added comment that the one who was expected has arrived is natural. It is just the sort of announcement that a neighbor would make when the children come home for Christmas.

Commandment/gospel is a particularly difficult form of dialectic. A sermon which runs "Thou shalt not steal, but Jesus loves thieves" can go wrong in several ways. Both assertions are true, but if improperly combined, both can be lost. It must be made clear that it is the same God who commands and loves. Above all, the dialectic between the two must be joined in the lives of the hearers. When a thief has truly heard the commandment, that thief is also, just then, very ready to hear that Jesus loves thieves. Care must also be taken so that the two words don't appear to complement one another. Then the message amounts to something like this, "Jesus loves thieves but he would love you even more if you weren't one." The love of Jesus is cheapened, and he is made to appear as a calculating school principal.

I recently had the privilege of hearing a fine sermon on the divorce text from Matthew 19. Divorce was clearly presented as something forbidden by God's commands. The preacher didn't weasel on this text. The preacher nicely joined the dialectic in the lives of the hearers. Divorced people, and there were some in the congregation, were not excused. The "no" was there for them to hear. A sad and difficult experience in their lives was raised to the surface of consciousness. Those hearers who, by thought or act, have contributed to the reality of divorce were also directly addressed. The command was made clear and brisk in their hearing. But also, as to those broken by law, the word of the gospel was clearly spoken. The preacher didn't forget how, in the New Testament, the word of Jesus' comfort rings for those who have great need. The dialectic was not only full of life, but the parts were never presented as complementary.

The observer may ask, "But doesn't this dialectic offer the hearer an easy way out? Doesn't it suggest to the hearer that it is just fine to get a divorce because God forgives sinners anyway?" No. That can only happen when the message is thought of as a static, fixed word within which one can maneuver. When the oral word is spoken, it is either heard in faith or not. There really isn't time for maneuvering.

Commandment-gospel dialectic is important. It is particularly difficult, and care must be taken by the preacher so that both the components are not lost. The time has come to turn to the most common form of dialectic, that of the juxtaposition of the offense of the gospel and the gospel itself.

THE GOSPEL AND ITS OFFENSE

There is no more important theological perspective for preaching in general and dialectic in particular than that of the offense of the gospel. When the gospel is thought of as a fixed datum, a delivered proposition, its offense is not readily apparent. It can be considered from a distance and adjusted as needed. But when one thinks of the gospel as an urgent word of communication, life shows us clearly enough that it can be heard as an offense. Just as a kind word from a family member can, in certain circumstances, be heard as a word of bondage and hate, so it is with the loving word of Jesus. Not only is there an offense in the claim of the gospel upon the hearer, but an even greater offense in the way the gospel turns the necessary workings of the world upside down. The gospel's offense, that scandal of the positive, most often forms one side of the homiletical dialectic.

Consider, for instance, the potential offensiveness of the promise of Psalm 139. The psalm, with the exception of the final, somewhat bitter part, is about how the Lord knows us. One who is desperately lost would certainly be happy to be found by God through the words of this psalm, but here we consider the offense.

The Lord knows the human creature inside and out, private life as well as public. Before the Lord there are no secrets. God knows when we sit down and when we stand up. God even knows our thoughts before those inner words become articulated sounds. Before God, even the secrets of our identity, which we need in order to live, are plain as day.

Who wants to be known that well, so completely well? Who doesn't sometimes want to keep some measure of identity back, in reserve? The psalmist even anticipates our mortal desire to flee: "Whither shall I go from thy Spirit? Or whither shall I flee from thy presence?" There is no escape; not in aspirations or in shabby living, not in imagination, fancy, or even death. There is no escape from the Lord, period! That is the offense of the good news of Psalm 139.

All texts, once the gospel has been found, have their scandal. One wonders if it is fair to give all the workers a full wage, even the ones who haven't worked long. One wonders, as did Mary in the annunciation, just how God can accomplish what is promised when the conditions seem hopeless. One wonders, upon hearing that there is one door into the sheepfold, if it wouldn't be wise to leave some other options open, just in case. The gospel is an offense to the natural person. It is like someone whom you are deeply angry with being kind to you, genuinely kind. It's awful! The offense of the gospel and the word of the gospel itself most often form the two sides of homiletical dialectic.

The offense of the gospel, and there may be several, must be lifted to the surface of consciousness in the sermon. The offense must be clearly stated and shown, in dialectic with the gospel, to be an attempt to escape the good news and return to the law, the end of which is death. If the text is Psalm 139, our shame over being completely known by another must be faced. The solitary alternative, however, must be shown to be deep loneliness. Our almost pathological concern for identity might be lifted up, an identity which we do seek on both the heights and depths of human experience. Yet self-imposed identity always eludes us, fleeing just before our sure grasp, sending us plunging ahead for more and more. Our search is a way of being lost.

The offense of the gospel is most arresting when it is lifted to the surface of consciousness in a subtle but deep way. After all, the preacher is by no means trying to push the hearer into a certain condition, but to lift to the surface some wariness of the gospel which is already there. The preacher does well to be aware of the basic rules of rhetoric. If, in speaking of the offense of the gospel, the preacher is too abrupt, too aggressive on the attack, hearers will simply turn their attention away. People, for their own good, sometimes need to be approached with rhetorical cunning. Even Amos, who can hardly be considered a model of subtlety, didn't start right in on Israel. He approached them by way of their neighbors. In everyday conversation, certain preliminaries are appropriate before a difficult message is to be brought.

Subtlety should not be had at the expense of depth. At some point in the sermon, the offense of the promise should take on depth for the hearer. For example, a discussion of the nature of forgiveness may not have great personal depth for the participants. Greater depth is gained when the hearer is reminded how difficult it is to forgive. The greatest depth comes with knowledge of the scandal of being forgiven. A sermon cannot have the same personal urgency throughout. It is sometimes shallow, perhaps even a little humorous, but only so that depth may eventually be gained. Schiller said that the "art of rhetoric is the art of the placement of lights"—lights which, along the avenue of the sermon, should vary in their intensity.

Clear, no-strings-attached preaching of the gospel is the other side of the dialectic. Preaching the promise is the most difficult part of the homiletical craft—difficult because it's so easy to hedge the gospel in with qualifications, and difficult because promise language tends to become airborne, ethereal, and detached from life.

Special care should be taken to avoid "if . . . then" constructions when preaching the promise. People never outgrow their need to hedge the gospel in the direction of their own virtues, and so our vigil against good news which is really spoken as timid exhortation must never lapse.

Some "if . . . then" constructions of the gospel are obvious violations of the nature of Christ's gift: "*If* you could just do a little better as church members, *then* Jesus would love you more," or "*If* you could be more obedient to the law, *then* Jesus would reward you with the peace that passes all understanding." Other "if . . . then" constructions are subtle and more difficult to remove: "*If* you exercise greater responsibility as citizens, *then* God will reward you with a greater share of Christ's freedom," or "*If* we love one another, *then* Jesus will certainly be better able to love us." Some subtle "if . . . then" statements are pious sounding and even biblical: "*If* you only can believe, *then* you will be saved." The latter statement is most certainly biblical and true, but when presented as a demand for faith apart from the author and focus of belief, the statement is devastating for consciences. Preachers find innumerable ways to attach strings to the gospel, for the simple declaration of grace is nearly always accompanied with the suspicion that something really needs to be held back so the world, and even the church, can be preserved. The gospel always seems to go too far.

The language of the commandment or of the offense of the promise is often brisk, concrete, and down-to-earth, whereas the language of the gospel is often artificial and otherworldly. Severe linguistic contrasts are always difficult for the ear to adjust to; and when language is airborne, the gospel, as a communication event, is pulled away from the life of the hearer. Gospel language must be just as brisk, concrete, and down-to-earth as was the cross. Language clues can be taken from the offense of the sermon, using the same concretizations to show the contrast with the gospel. Just as the dialectic is joined in the life of the hearer, so also the language of the two parts of the dialectic should be similar, even though the parts are kept utterly distinct.

Psalm 139:11–12 provides us with a little paradigm for a good sermon. There is dialectic, with corresponding language, and a clear statement of promise. "If I say, 'Let only darkness cover me, and the light about me be night,' even the darkness is not dark to thee, the night is bright as the day; for darkness is as light with thee." Dull darkness is where the psalmist longs to be—that nether region where visions cannot be seen or responsibility noticed. Yet God sees through the gloom and straight into the heart. God knows and still loves. That verse cries out to the Christian preacher for some word of Jesus and the cross.

PROBLEMS WITH DIALECTIC

The use of law-gospel dialectic in preaching is risky. So many things can go wrong, and when they do go wrong, everything may be lost. Even a poor educational sermon retains some value, but when a pastor preaches a sermon where dialectic has gone completely haywire, hearers are badly served. Not only is the management of dialectic difficult, just as law and gospel is a perspective which one can never completely master, but there are particular problems which are endemic to its use.

The structure of a dialectic sermon may become routine and utterly predictable. Predictability can creep into any type of sermon, but in this case it is the result of method as well as personal habit. When the shape of the sermon is the same week after week and the hearers start to think, "Now it's soon time for the gospel," all is lost. The only cure is imagination. Preachers simply cannot be afraid to try to be creative about sermon composition. Dialectical structure is remarkably durable, though. When a parishioner thinks, "Now it's soon time for the gospel," it is more often a sign that the sermon is not being done well than that the method is faulty. "The Trumpet Shall Sound" comes at the same place in every performance of Handel's *Messiah*, but when performed well, it is always new and captivating.

In a dialectical sermon, the commandment or the offense of the gospel can easily take the form of an attack upon the hearer. "Thou shalt not steal" becomes an impassioned scolding, a relentless homiletical vendetta against the hearer rather than a clear statement of God's law and the obvious reasons for its worth. It is as though a rhetorical cudgel is being used to push the listeners farther and farther into the pit so that the gospel can come and wonderfully pluck them out. Such heavy-handed use of the law demonstrates a lack of homiletical sensitivity. Commandments do show us our need for grace but always as a word of God which has its own power. Parishioners can tell when a sermon takes on the character of a personal or homiletical vendetta.

When the offense of the gospel is used as an attack, the results are even worse. God's capacity to see into the heart becomes a law rather than an offense for our salvation, and the master's generosity becomes a pattern for living rather than a gift that challenges our expectations of God. The freedom of the text as a communication event which can be heard as law is destroyed by the preacher's insistence on providing that law. The offense may seem to the hearer to complement the gospel, instead of being stated as the other side or escape from it. People don't need to be softened up for the gospel, because the saving word of Jesus both does away with the old person and brings forth the new. The gospel cannot be the hand of law pushing down while the hand of love lifts up, but one hand lifting up.

Charges of manipulation have been leveled against pastors using the dialectic of law and gospel. The only answer to that charge is "yes" and "no." All Christian preachers who are intent on the gospel's being heard seek to manipulate the hearer in the direction of the promise even though hearing the gospel, as a work of the Spirit, cannot be guaranteed. Actually, everything depends on the manipulation being done well, for the moment the hearer has a sense of being tugged along, all is lost. All oral discourse is polemical, an invasion of the privacy, the solitude, the individuality of the other. Who wants to be a person whose conversation doesn't ever encounter or affect anyone?

All our words are endlessly manipulative, and even when they are words of love, there is some bondage in them. Only the words of the grace of Jesus are not manipulative, for they give true freedom.

Dialectic is not the only rhetorical form that preachers can use. Most preachers who preach on a weekly basis learn to vary the fabric of their sermons in order to avoid being bored and creating boredom. Dialectic is difficult, as has been readily confessed, but thankfully not as difficult as any formal discussion makes it seem. Because of its oral roots, dialectic is as near as our common speech. Even though it is tricky, dialectic sometimes provides just the right context for the gospel to ring. That makes any difficulty and risk worthwhile.

Conclusion

We have sought to provide a discussion of the crisis of language within society in general and the church in particular. Most Christians understand the church to be an oral community, a community which is especially threatened by the decay and denial of the spoken word. Scripture is not the source of language crisis. The Bible demonstrates a keen sense for the power of oral communication, and Jesus himself is called the Word of God.

Because language is constitutive of community, its misuse and decay must be considered a preeminent manifestation of sin. We, as usual, are the problem. Traces of the struggle against orality can be found in the sight-sound split that has accompanied printing and made our age highly visual. Preaching in particular and the oral character of the church in general suffer when people assume that "seeing is believing." But the Christian pastor is called to a ministry of the Word. Pastors preach and parishioners bear witness because of the command of Jesus and the nature of the gospel. New life can be gained for interpretation and preaching by reflecting on the way the language of the Word of God works.

Church history has been characterized by growth and expansion. Kenneth Scott Latourette observed that mission is the key whereby the history of Christianity in the West is best understood. Christian mission was certainly energized by many factors, but who can deny a central place to preaching? Now the church in the West seems terribly settled. For the first time, Western Christianity is fighting against the

105

prevailing winds and has fallen back a step or two. How tempting it is, in such a time, for churches to assume a protective posture, turning in to conserve whatever energy is left.

We shouldn't worry about the survival of Christianity: that is God's business. Pastors remain called, however, to the ministry of the Word. A primary element in that ministry is the clear proclamation of the gospel, both for those who are baptized and those who are not. Perhaps our Lord Jesus will not deny us a slight sense of the heroism of our task. After all, who wants to be a part of an organism composing itself for a suitable death?

Preaching is a difficult business, a craft which is in no wise held in esteem by the public these days. Yet, week in and week out, faith is awakened and sustained through dedicated preachers. I think of them as a noble, if tattered and often discouraged company, one which I am proud to call my own. Our Lord Jesus has used his word to call forth the church in the past and will continue to do so. A renewed sense of the power of that word in the preaching of the church will not lead us into complacency, but will help us take our task even more seriously.

People really do come to hear. They are expectant of the sermon, if only for a little while. They come with various concerns: with the impetuosity of youth or the wisdom of years, giddy with popularity or nursing the wound of a broken friendship, flushed with satisfying labor or bending beneath some desultory task, filled with exuberant hopes or shattered dreams. Above all, parishioners come afraid of an ominous future, wondering if there is any saving voice from beyond. Pastors are called to preach the word of the gospel to them, and they are called to demand good preaching of us. Let it be our prayer and our labor that we do not fail.

Notes

---

1. THE CHURCH AND
THE PROBLEM OF LANGUAGE

1. Gerhard Ebeling, *Luther* (Philadelphia: Fortress Press, 1970), 131–2.

2. Ernest Käsemann, *New Testament Questions of Today* (London: SCM Press, 1969), 288.

3. Gerard Manley Hopkins, "Pied Beauty," *The Poems* (New York and London: Oxford University Press, 1970), 69.

4. Gerhard Ebeling, *Introduction to a Theological Theory of Language* (Philadelphia: Fortress Press, 1973), 77.

5. Ibid., 116.

2. WORDS AND THE
WORD IN OUR CULTURE

1. James Robinson and John Cobb, eds., *The New Hermeneutic* (New York: Harper & Row, 1964), 2:123.

2. Susan Langer, *Philosophy in a New Key* (Cambridge: Harvard University Press, 1978), 110.

3. Walter Ong, *The Presence of the Word* (New Haven and London: Yale University Press, 1967), 143.

4. Langer, *Philosophy*, 128–29.

5. Ibid., 129–32.

6. Ibid., 136.

7. Ibid., 139.

8. Harold Strahmer, "Speak That I May See Thee" (New York: Macmillan Co., 1968), 15.

9. Ibid., 17.

10. Ibid., 43.

11. Plato, *The Republic*, trans. H. D. Lee (Harmondsworth and Baltimore: Penguin Books, 1955), 383.

12. Ong, *Presence*, 215.

13. Ernst Cassier, *The Philosophy of Symbolic Forms* (New Haven: Yale University Press, 1967), 27.

14. Ong, *Presence*, 21.

15. Ibid., 19.

16. Ibid., 21.

17. Ibid., 84.

18. Ibid., 45.

19. Ibid., 71.

20. Ibid., 89.

3. THE RESOURCES

1. Ebeling, *Luther*, 13–26.

2. Paul Tillich, *A History of Christian Thought* (London: SCM Press, 1968), 228.

3. The polemical character of Luther's writing is nowhere more evident than in the vitriolic title of this treatise. The modern reader is often puzzled and offended by the fighting character of Luther's works, a polemic repaid in full by his enemies. One must remember, however, that Luther took theology very seriously, as did his opponents. Even if it can't save you, theology is crucial to keeping the avenues of the gospel unclogged. Luther also lived at the beginning of the burgeoning world of print. He was still very much a part of a highly oral culture, and oral cultures are polemical by nature. Human speech is always something of an invasion of another's privacy.

4. *Luther's Works*, ed. Eric Gritsch (Philadelphia: Fortress Press, 1970), 39:175.

5. Ibid., 180.

6. Ibid., 181.

7. Eric Gritsch and Robert Jenson, *Lutheranism* (Philadelphia: Fortress Press, 1976), 42–43.

8. Ibid., 44.

9. Clyde Fant, *Bonhoeffer: Worldly Preaching* (Camden, N.J.: Thomas Nelson & Sons, 1975), 126.

10. Amos Wilder, *Early Christian Rhetoric* (Cambridge: Harvard University Press, 1964), 6.

11. Gerhard von Rad, *Old Testament Theology* (Edinburgh: Oliver & Boyd, 1965), 2:80–98.

12. Raymond Brown, *The Gospel According to John* (Garden City, N.Y.: Doubleday & Co., 1966), 24.

13. Fredrick W. Danker, *Jesus and the New Age* (St. Louis: Clayton, 1972), xvi.

14. Robinson and Cobb, *New Hermeneutic*, 115.

15. Walter F. Otto, *The Homeric Gods* (New York: Pantheon Books, 1954), 123.

16. Ibid., 107.

4. THE WORD IN THE CHURCH'S LIFE

1. Gritsch and Jenson, *Lutheranism*, 82.

2. Martin Buber, *The Knowledge of Man* (London: George Allen & Unwin, 1965), 112.

3. Gritsch and Jenson, *Lutheranism*, 44.